UNSTUCK

*Move from Powerless to Empowered
in Your Relationships*

CHARLENE BENSON

*Candy & Mark
Here's a map for your
road trip?
Charlene
Benson*

ILLUMIFY MEDIA GLOBAL
Littleton, Colorado

UNSTUCK

Published by
Illumify Media Global
www.IllumifyMedia.com
"Write. Publish. Market. *SELL!*"

Library of Congress Control Number: 2019912463

Paperback ISBN: 978-1-949021-39-4
eBook ISBN: 978-1-949021-40-0

Typeset by Art Innovations (http://artinnovations.in/)
Cover design by Debbie Lewis

Printed in the United States of America

DEDICATION

Dedicated to HBHS Class of 1970 for unwittingly
prophesying over me.
"Charlene has finally crawled out of the ditch,
and is having another wild party."
That's right! Only this one is a kingdom celebration!

CONTENTS

ACKNOWLEDGMENTS

I'm deeply grateful to the following for helping me complete this book:

To God for inspiration, for continuing to lead me into deeper understanding of relationship dynamics, and for helping me overcome the fear of writing a book. He truly is "the author and finisher of our faith" (and all the projects He gives us to do). Hebrews 12:2 (KJV)

To my husband, Mike, the sand in my oyster. (I'm the sand in his oyster, too). I could not have come out of my ditch without his help, nor could he have made it out of his without my help.

To my sons, Steve and Dave, for turning out to be awesome kids despite all the mistakes we made as parents.

To my daughters-in-law, Melissa and Katie, for their support, love, and acceptance.

To my grandchildren in heaven, on earth, and yet to be born, for bringing me such joy.

To my editors, for all the hours you spent editing. Conni Griffee, special thanks for your words of encouragement and validation! Heather Vigil, for helping and teaching me to be a better writer through suggestions and corrections. Ginny Dissette and Carolee Wise for corrections and suggestions.

To Illumify: Mike Klassen for agreeing to publish my work, Karen Scalf Bouchard for being an *awesome* book coach and editor, Alissa

McGowan and Geoff Stone for copy editing, Jennifer Clark for her help and support, Debbie Lewis for the cover design and Erin Grantham for helping to navigate the social media world.

To the people who cheered me on and encouraged me to write this book: Linda Splan, for reading my first rough draft, Conni Griffee, Carolee Wise, Amy Heitzman-Leigh, 5th Generation World Race Squad 0 (and their parents), Pam Dice and Pete Averson, Dana Whitney, Marcus and Lorena Ward, June Hale, Christina Kwak, Melanie King, Alley Hawthorne, Patrick Carnes, Gina and Aaron Hafer, and Sarah at JC Penney for taking my cover photo.

To my peer groups: Mary Murray, Kathy Narum, Jennifer Sleek,and Abigail Esquivel, Jennifer Diebel, and Jennifer Mone'.

To all my clients, who have taught me so much, inspired me to develop these ideas and use them to aid in their journeys, and encouraged me to write this book.

To my friends, those we hang around and go camping with, from SSA, from school, college, grad school, church, groups, Mini-Tap, and all the people we've met from traveling the US, through AIM, and throughout the world. Thank you for the ways you have touched my life.

To my relatives: Thank you for the ways you have positively influenced my life. To my deceased parents who taught me many things.

To my church: Flatirons Church leaders, my Deaf friends, interpreter friends, Shift leaders, and fellow step-study and group participants. Also, my former church, WCG, where I learned the Bible, became grounded in truth, and learned to value travel.

To Azmera: Christina Carter for giving me the opportunity to present the Ditch People model in Kenya, Costa Rica, and Cyprus.

To Writers who helped me: Mary Murray and Kirsten Wilson for inviting me to be a part of their writing group, for their feedback and encouragement. To Kirsten for introducing me to Writers' Boot Camp, Margaret Feinberg and Jonathan Merritt; and Writers on the Rock, Dave Rupert, Amy Young, and staff for help, support, and encouragement. Marla Benroth for leading the North Metro Writer's group. Shelly Hitz for encouragement and tools for writers to get their works published.

To Brant Hansen on page 92 of *Blessed are the Misfits*, for giving me a compelling reason to complete this book. I want people to know a better way to cope instead of allowing fear and powerlessness to devastate families.

To all the people referenced in the book, and to the people I love, for the examples they provide. Their names have been changed to protect the innocent and guilty.

Special thanks to Rob Scuka and the late Bernard Guerney for developing Relationship Enhancement (RE) communication skills for couples and to Don and Alexandra Flecky for making available online those tools that transformed the way my husband and I interact with one another. Many of the ideas in this book spawned from what I learned from RE.

INTRODUCTION

Are you stuck in a relationship ditch?

Let's find out. Check the boxes that apply to you:

☐ It seems like I'm walking on eggshells around my partner.
☐ Sometimes I feel manipulated and controlled.
☐ I often have to give up what I really want.
☐ I feel frustrated in my relationships.
☐ I often feel obligated and resentful.
☐ I am disappointed by unmet expectations.
☐ It's difficult for me to express how I really feel.
☐ I'm often angry.
☐ Sometimes people accuse me of being controlling.

If you checked more than a box or two, this book is for you.

IMAGINE TWO PARALLEL DITCHES RUNNING ALONGSIDE A ROAD

Relationships tend to be made up of opposites: "others-focused" and "me-focused" people with different default behaviors. Polarizing of positions results, creating even greater behavioral extremes and driving people farther apart. This is true in marriages and in other relationships as well.

When extreme default behaviors are keeping partners stuck and distanced from each other, it's like "being stuck in a ditch." Imagine two deep ditches running parallel on opposite sides of a road. When you're stuck in a rut on one side of the road, and your partner is mired in the ditch on the other, it's hard to come together. It's hard to move forward.

On the other hand, learning to reign in extreme default behaviors can turn an exhausting, difficult relationship into a true partnership. When two people can recognize and stop their polarizing behaviors—then get and stay on the road—they really do have a chance of moving forward in a balanced relationship characterized by healthy choices.

And that's what I hope to help you achieve.

I'VE LIVED THE "BEFORE" AND "AFTER"

I know about the pain of this kind of relationship dynamic firsthand. Most of my life I felt stuck. Frequently, I either felt like I didn't have a choice, or the available options seemed unacceptable. Any direction I looked, it seemed that unhappiness stared me in the face. I felt trapped, as if I were stuck in a deep ditch!

Often, I felt controlled by my husband and viewed him as selfish and manipulative. He could easily talk me out of doing what I wanted and into doing what he wanted. The truth is, he could control and manipulate me because I didn't know any other way to respond. I gave in easily and didn't hold my ground.

It was as if some of my boundaries were on hinges. He'd march up to them and push through them with little or no resistance from me. Then I'd blame him for crossing the lines I'd drawn but couldn't enforce myself. Unaware of my part in *allowing his behavior*, I was quick to cave in and give up my position.

Sometimes I still struggle with that. For example, I'm looking for a new vehicle, and a Ford Explorer seems ideal. It's acceptable in every way, except it only gets 18 miles per gallon. My husband has suggested other models that get better gas mileage.

There's wisdom in what he's saying. At the same time, the old tape running in my head says, "*Here he goes again, blocking me from getting what I really want.*" Indeed, it *feels* like he's trying to talk me out of what I want . . . again! And even though I know now that's not his motivation, it's surprising how quick I am to question myself: "Am I too willing to give up on my wishes because he's pointing me in another direction? For that matter, what *do* I really want?" And in the wake of questions like these, I can lose touch with my own feelings. I have to work hard in order to recognize and name my own emotions.

These are the same old patterns that defined our relationship for many years: patterns we've—thankfully!—replaced with others that are healthier, balanced, and life-giving.

Now that I'm aware of my old template, I try to evaluate how I feel inside instead of blindly defaulting to his recommendation. I also try to consider his point of view without automatically resorting to old defenses. In other words, at the same time I recognize that my yearnings are just as important as other factors, I acknowledge that his motivation is to be helpful instead of controlling.

It's a balanced mindset that is nothing short of life changing.

And I know it can change your life, too.

MY EXTREME BEHAVIORS DIDN'T START IN MY MARRIAGE

Looking back on my childhood, I see key factors influencing my reactions and ways of relating. I believe many of these factors stemmed from having an easily triggered, angry dad, and a people-pleasing, emotionally shut-down mom.

I don't say these things to judge my parents, my husband, or even myself. Unhealthy ways of relating can be passed down for generations and are pervasive in almost every family. We are told not to judge in Matthew 7:1, which includes not judging ourselves or our families.

Nevertheless, had I known or understood how my past affected my present-day decisions, I would not have walked or waited; I would have run to get help to deal with my woundedness. However, common attitudes of my era prevailed: attitudes that said, "Don't air your dirty laundry in front of others." or "Only crazy people need counseling." So, I never went to therapy. The patterns that got passed down to me were repeated by me. Both my husband and I copied our parents' ways, except how we interacted was just different enough from our parents that neither of us picked up on the similarities.

It took me thirty years after leaving my family of origin to get help. That means there were decades in which to make a lot of bad decisions! These decisions were based on inherited lies, fears, and negative beliefs, which got imbedded because of how I interpreted my experiences, how I internalized what others said to or about me, and the conclusions I made based on things that happened to me.

Of course, at the time I didn't understand how I was being influenced by what I experienced and believed during my childhood. I only knew that I felt unlovable and unacceptable; and I was convinced that if anyone knew the *real* me, they would reject me on the spot. At the same time, I desperately sought love despite the fact that I didn't consciously know that's what I was seeking, didn't know what love even looked like, and subconsciously believed it existed outside of my reach.

That's a recipe for failure for sure.

But that didn't stop me.

I was a poster child for "clueless."

Perhaps, like me, you've spent decades making "choices" that were driven by your past—without even realizing it.

But here's the good news: It's never too late to change. I'm proof of that. And I know that the principles that worked for me can work for you, too.

In the following chapters, I'm going to help you recognize extreme default behaviors—in you and in other people in your life, too. I'm going to show you how to address the root of those behaviors. And I'm going to reveal how to change your "default" and consistently win at choosing healthier behaviors.

Are you ready to take control of the wheel of your own life?

Great. Let's get out of the ditch and back on the road.

CHAPTER 1

THE OTHERS-FOCUSED DITCH

"If you try to please all, you please none."
—Aesop

I woke up in a dark place. I didn't know how I got there or how I'd get out. Dazed and confused, I looked around, assessing my surroundings. The reality and gravity of the situation hit me all at once: I was stuck in a ditch!

I first became aware of my ditch behavior after an experience I had shopping at Home Goods (and, no, I didn't discover it in the "Ditch Decor" section, or in the "Trench Trinkets" aisle).

Here's the defining moment that woke me up:

Browsing through items lining the shelves, my eye caught a sculpted silk plant. I picked it up and wondered: *Would my husband like this? What would he think about it? How would he feel if I brought this home? He might not like it. He probably will think it's frivolous. I'm sure he will be upset if I spend money on this. He'd rather I save the money for something more practical.*

Replacing the silk plant on the shelf, I walked out of the store empty handed.

That was my typical thought pattern. But what happened next changed everything.

Driving home, something clicked. With a massive "Aha!" it dawned on me that, standing in Home Goods holding that silk plant, every single thought in my head had been about what I thought my husband would want. What would *he* think? Would *he* like it? How would *he* feel if I decided to buy this? What concerns would arise for *him*? Is this something *he* desires?

Not one aspect of my reasoning touched on what I thought or desired.

At that moment, I realized my evaluation process needed a major overhaul.

That day, I discovered a flaw in the criteria I used to make choices. I had left out how I felt and ignored what I wanted! While it is important to take into consideration what my spouse wants and how he feels about my decisions, my own feelings about any topic hold equal importance. Unfortunately, I hadn't been raised to think that way, and I had already lived many decades convinced that what I felt or wanted didn't matter.

Let me give you an everyday example of what this looked like in our lives:

Let's say my husband felt like seeing a movie. He'd ask me, "Do you want to go to a movie?"

Seems like a simple question, right? But instead of answering the actual question—did I want to see a movie?—I would begin a frantic monologue in my head that would go something like this: *He is asking me that question because obviously he wants to see that movie. I'm not interested in seeing that flick, but that's clearly what he wants to do, and he might get upset if I don't say yes.*

"Yes," I'd respond.

I would feel obligated. I might even feel resentful that he didn't suggest a movie I'd like to see. Mind you, I wouldn't breathe a word about my desire to see a different movie. The lie I believed back then was that if he really loved me, he'd know what I wanted. But exactly how was that supposed to happen? I have no idea. Some call it "magical thinking." I think I assumed he could read my mind. It only took me about thirty-five years to realize he couldn't!

But after my experience at Home Goods, I felt fed up with my situation and his lack of ability as a mind-reader. So, I started looking for a better way. In the process, awareness began to creep into my consciousness, much like the morning light invades the darkness: silently, stealthily, imperceptibly, slowly, relentlessly.

And what I discovered surprised me!

21 "OTHERS-FOCUSED" DEFAULT BEHAVIORS

First, I became conscious of certain behaviors I practiced.

These were my go-to responses to my husband and to other people, too. When I forced myself to be honest about these behaviors, I had to admit that I had embraced them because I felt powerless to receive love and acceptance. In other words, I was defaulting to these 21 reactions in a pathetic attempt to win favor and affection.

Here are the 21 behaviors I discovered in myself. I call them "Others-Focused"—or OF—behaviors. Do any sound familiar to you?

1. People-Pleasing

I was a people pleaser to an extreme degree. I tried hard to make others happy and rushed to help in any way I could.

Now, part of me truly enjoys serving others and—when in balance—this is a good and healthy trait to possess.

But the equilibrium gets off kilter when I do things to make other people happy while ignoring how it negatively affects me. Or when I do something I don't want to do and then resent the other person because I felt obligated.

One time while friends were visiting, my friend asked her daughter to pull her hair back. Immediately I hopped up and ran to get a hair tie. No one had asked me to do that. And that wasn't my job, anyway. Yes, I wanted to be helpful, but why? If I could have been honest with myself at the time, I would have admitted that I was being overly helpful out of a desire to be liked, accepted, and loved. What seemed like a nice gesture on the surface was actually rooted in my self-serving subconscious desire for approval.

Saying or doing what we think other people want in order to avoid conflict is another aspect of people-pleasing. Think of the nearly-cliché example of a young person who tries to please her parents and ends up miserable in business school rather than attending the art institute she preferred.

Not wanting to disappoint others or not knowing how to disagree in a non-confrontational way, we can go along with the wishes or viewpoints of others to keep the peace or make them happy.

And I had practiced this behavior for so many years, it became elevated it to an art form.

2. Defaulting to "Yes"

In the past, if someone asked me to do something or if my husband wanted something, my automatic response was, "Yes." Even if I took some time to think about it, my answer would still usually end up being "Yes." That was my default reaction based on my faulty reasoning process. I had been programmed to be compliant. Sometimes, after "Yes" fell out of my mouth, I'd think, *Oh, no! What did I just get myself into?!* And I would realize too late I'd once again committed myself to something I didn't want to do.

3. Readily Giving Up What I Wanted

Driven to seek approval, I was quick to relinquish what I wanted. I quickly gave up my preferences to satisfy the desires of others. I made their concerns my concerns and sought to fulfill their desires. Most of the time, it didn't occur to me to include my desires in the equation. If I wanted Chinese food for dinner and someone else mentioned Italian, guess where we'd end up? Giovanni's. (In case you're wondering, that's not a Chinese restaurant.)

From childhood onward, I became easily dissuaded from what I wanted to do by the disparaging remarks made by others, such as: "Why would you want to do that?" "That's too hard for you." "Why do you want to go?" "You can't do that anyway." "You never get anything right." "How are you going to pay for that?" Instead of standing up for what I wanted, most of the time I just gave up my desires without a fight. Because of that, I felt controlled.

After Mom died, Dad sold the farm and I helped him move to his second wife's home. At the time, he was getting rid of most of his furnishings. I asked, "Can I have your old refrigerator for our garage?"

His response was, "You don't want that."

Because of his negative reply and tone and my ingrained readiness to give up, I didn't pursue the fridge, even though I really did want it.

Why in the world did I so quickly default to what other people decided I wanted instead of knowing what I wanted for myself?

Julia Roberts's character in the movie *Runaway Bride* provides a classic example of this behavior. Whatever style of eggs each boyfriend preferred became her default choice as well. If someone she was dating liked poached eggs, that's what she'd order. If her next boyfriend preferred omelets, she'd eat omelets, too. In the movie, she finally realized she had no idea what kind of eggs she really did like. She had become so conditioned to letting other people define her choices.

I realized I was doing the exact same thing. If asked for my preference, my common response repertoire included: "It doesn't matter to me." "Whatever you want." "I don't care, you pick." "I don't know." "I'll have whatever you have."

4. Difficulty Making Decisions

I also had a hard time making decisions. One time, we went to Baskin Robbins at about 9:00 p.m. on a summer day. No one else was around. By the time I decided on the flavor I wanted, a line had formed and snaked out the door! My habit of ignoring what I wanted and focusing on the wants of others resulted in an inability to be decisive. I didn't know what I really wanted or how to decide on anything because I was so used to deferring to the preferences of those around me.

Once Julia Roberts's character became aware that she habitually deferred to the inclinations of the men she dated, it took a while for her to figure out her own tastes. The next scene shows her trying out different ways of making eggs for breakfast to determine her own preferences. Likewise, it took me a while to figure out what I favored. From time to time, I still struggle to discern if I'm just going along with the crowd or if it's what I truly want for myself. But now I'm aware of my indecision and consciously think about it.

5. Walking on Eggshells

Speaking of eggs, I often felt like I walked on eggshells. In trying to ascertain exactly what my significant other wanted, I lived with uncertainty and insecurity. *If I say or do this, will he get upset with me? What if I do that? He'll probably not like that either.* I tried hard to keep him from getting bothered with me.

Somehow the chicken got out of the egg, because I became a "master feather smoother." I spent a lot of time attempting to appease his anger.

I never picked up on the truth until recently. And that truth is simply this: These tactics of trying to please others or prevent others from getting upset with me rarely worked!

6. Difficulty Expressing Thoughts and Feelings

For many years, I had a hard time expressing how I felt. I emulated my mom's pattern of holding in her feelings, especially if they were negative, until she exploded. That didn't happen often, but I remember a couple of times when she did go toe-to-toe with my dad on some issue. It makes me wonder how many generations ago that started because I would do the same thing. I let my hurts pile up until I couldn't stand the pain and frustration anymore and then let my spouse have it with both barrels.

Shortly after I got married, something my husband did upset me. When he asked what was wrong, I tersely retorted, "Nothing."

He tried so hard to get me to share what was eating at me, but I *could not* tell him. The subconscious message that got passed down to me as a young girl was too ingrained. *Your feelings don't count.* Because I believed that lie, I lived as though it was true for most of my life. I could not muster the courage to express how I truly felt because that belief held such a strong grip on me! Over the years, I've seen many others silenced by the same lie.

I'm much better at expressing my feelings now, but it has been one of the toughest behaviors to overcome. It has been especially difficult because my significant other is so vocal and forthright about his feelings and opinions that I often feel engulfed by them and unable to express my own.

7. Avoiding Conflict

Attempting to prevent disagreements and conflicts, I tended toward avoidance. That was the model I witnessed growing up and replicated as an adult. If I thought my spouse would be upset with something I did, I just didn't say anything about it. If I anticipated that we wouldn't see eye-to-eye on a matter, I'd postpone the discussion for as long as possible. If I purchased something I thought he wouldn't like, I would bring it home when he wasn't around and a wait for a couple of weeks to use the new item. If he commented, "When did you get that?" I'd remark, "This? Oh, I've had it for a while." That was how I avoided confrontation. And I *thought* I was being honest!

8. Co-Dependence

Co-dependence is just a fancy word for oscillating between trying to get someone to do what you want in an indirect manner and simultaneously trying to make that person happy or prevent an angry outburst. In the past, either I would compromise what I wanted and feel resentful about that, or I would try to control the situation and behavior of others in an indirect way. I'd attempt to avoid ruffling feathers while trying to manage my world at the same time.

In order to feel okay about myself, I have realized, I needed others to like me. I had low self-esteem and did not value myself or believe I was worthy. Deep down, I believed I was unlovable and was terrified that if anyone knew the real me, I'd be rejected. I worked hard for acceptance, which got in the way of having solid boundaries. In an effort to get along, I'd laugh at off-colored jokes I didn't think were funny, go places I didn't really want to go, eat food I didn't like, and keep quiet about what I really thought and felt. In truth, I valued the thoughts and feelings of others so much that they drowned out my own. Looking back, now that I think about it, often I truly didn't know how I felt.

9. Blaming

Blaming others came naturally to me. I held others responsible for my stuck situation, deserving or not. I blamed my spouse for all sorts of things, including controlling me, not taking me into consideration, and being self-centered.

Mired deep in my ditch, I didn't see my own issues. In my mind, everything was *his* fault! Of course, some of the blame was warranted because no one is perfect, but I got hung up on the truth of that. His wrongdoing was evident to me, but I could not see my part at all. Blinded, I believed I was innocent in the matter, whatever it was, and I felt self-righteously justified in blaming my husband for everything.

Sadly, I missed seeing the role I played in the situation. Because I couldn't see how my actions contributed to our impasse, I stayed powerless, waiting for him to do something to change my predicament. Little did I know how empowering it can be to take a hard look at our own behaviors and attitudes. Those, we can change!

10. Being Passive

In my relationship with my spouse, I tended to be passive. I'd go along with whatever he wanted. Most of the time I truly didn't care. The belief that I didn't get a choice lay at the root of my passivity, outside the reach of my awareness. I had been conditioned to give priority to what everyone else wanted.

This carried over into friendships as well. In adulthood, when I'd get together with friends (who tended to be like me), our discussion about something as simple as where to go to eat looked like this:

Friend: "Where do you want to go for dinner?"

Me: "I don't know. Where do you want to go?"

Occasionally, I'd timidly offer an option followed by a quick caveat that we could go somewhere else if they wanted, rarely advocating for my desires or opinions.

My mom and other key women in my life provided the model for how I learned to approach others, especially men. Often, Mom beat around the bush or hinted at what she wanted. "That restaurant looks interesting." (Implying that's where she wanted to go). "That necklace is really pretty." (Hinting that is something she would like). "You don't suppose you could pick up some milk on the way home?" (Anticipating a protest or complaint). Notice how the topic is approached in a negative, indirect, I-don't-expect-you-to-do-what-I-want kind of way?

I didn't know this, but subconsciously, I was afraid to advocate for what I wanted, fearful that I'd be stepping on someone else's toes, or that my idea would be rejected. By default, I automatically deferred to the desires of others. I didn't even know why or what drove my responses. Nor did it occur to me to ponder the reason, either.

11. Feeling Obligated

Put simply, I often felt obligated. "I have to do this!" "I must take care of my family!" "I am responsible for taking care of everyone around me!" "I'm obligated to make sure everyone is comfortable!"

In the past, I didn't feel like I had a choice. I was like Martha in the Bible, who felt obligated to serve everyone (Luke 10:38–42). For some reason, it never occurred to me to question this. Nor did I think through how this affected me or my attitude. I never even considered how it influenced the way I reacted to others.

12. Feeling Resentful

Close on the heels of obligation comes resentment. When we don't want to do something but go ahead and do it anyway, resentment rears its ugly head. Because it feels like there's no choice, we can start to feel like a martyr, self-righteous and self-sacrificing.

I know in my life, I would often think, *I'm sacrificing so much, surely someone will notice and help me.* When that didn't happen, I resented those around me for not offering to help.

I hated feeling like I didn't have an option. I was bothered that tasks always seemed to fall on my shoulders. I became irritated at others for what I perceived to be self-centered on their part.

That kind of resentment can't help but leak out onto others, like an oil spill polluting the water of relationships.

13. Being Sarcastic

Often, my bottled-up feelings and resentments would slip out through sarcastic remarks. When my husband would come home later than expected, with just the right amount of self-righteous martyrdom in my tone, I'd spit out, "Well, it's about time you showed up."

I would avoid expressing my true feelings, which were that I was disappointed that he didn't call, sad from missing him, or afraid that something bad might have happened.

14. Being Critical and/or Gossipy

When I felt especially hurt, I criticized the things I didn't like about my husband, usually complaining to others without ever confronting him about my feelings. When I was stuck in the ditch of my own extreme default behaviors, it was all too easy to get hung up on the truth of his shortcomings.

This was a pattern I learned from my family growing up. My parents frequently pointed out my shortcomings and those of my siblings, while staying silent about what we did right. I suppose they assumed we knew when we were doing the right thing and only needed to be told when we weren't. Because I was criticized a lot as a child, I replicated that behavior.

Being critical of others is easy, because no one is perfect. The closer we get to others, the more glaring their flaws seem to be, especially if they mirror in some way the issues that we can't see in ourselves.

The more I focused on what I didn't like, the bigger my spouse's flaws became, and the quicker I forgot his positive qualities. That is a sure-fire way to unravel a relationship.

Like Peter who, when he walked on the water, allowed the waves to loom larger than Jesus, I let negative thoughts wash over me, and then I sank (Matthew 14:29–30). I had been trained to look for the negative, not understanding that what we focus on expands. Therefore, I continued to look at all my relationships through that critical lens.

15. Stuffing My Hurts

In our family growing up, my dad was the angry one. I stuffed my anger down, and then it leaked out sideways as hurt.

Before becoming aware, I didn't understand the difference between anger and hurt. Hurt tends to be directed inward, while anger projects outward. When someone hurt me, I'd feel sorry for myself and have my own little pity party where I was the only attendee. I discovered that hurt people tend to retaliate in passive-aggressive ways. When that doesn't work, it can lead to withdrawing, freezing, or shutting down.

I tended not to get angry at the people who were angry at me. Most of the time. I bottled up my emotion until it built up to the point of explosion. Then I'd dump all my frustration out at one time on my spouse, kids, or others whether they were deserving of my anger or not.

Some attempts to ease the hurt appear harmless, like occasionally reaching for a candy bar or other comfort food, working out excessively, or spending too much money. But other coping mechanisms can be more destructive, like reaching for another drink or drug, or cutting oneself. Masked hurt can also show up as depression, lethargy, and lack of motivation.

16. Being Passive-Aggressive

Passive-aggression is characterized by many of the other behaviors described already such as using sarcasm and complaining to others. The behavior is hurtful or disrespectful to the other, but not obvious. People who engage in passive-aggressive behavior feel like they have gotten secret revenge and avoided the retaliation that a direct confrontation would bring.

I've heard of some interesting examples of passive-aggressive behaviors. In one movie, a husband and wife are arguing on their way home from an event. He storms into the house, hangs up his coat, and stomps off to the living room. She follows behind, and with a grand gesture removes his coat from its hook, letting it drop in a pile on the floor.

Other classic passive-aggressive behaviors include pulling a partner's clothes out of the drawers and throwing them on the floor, purposely serving burnt toast, or saying yes to something but purposely avoiding completing the task.

17. Withdrawing

Because sharing feelings and expressing my perspective was so difficult for me, I found it much easier to withdraw than to stand up for what I wanted or needed. Frequently, I used the same tactic I saw my parents employ: sweep it under the rug and hope it goes away. Time often rendered the problem obsolete, which reinforced the illusion that this approach works. It doesn't!

There were certain issues that kept resurfacing and inevitably led to blow-ups. These were "hot buttons" in our relationship. That describes topics on which we disagreed that regularly reoccurred, caused escalated arguments, and never got resolved. After each time it happened, we retreated to our respective corners and licked our emotional wounds. We then avoided the issue until something triggered it again, when it would result in yet another argument that went nowhere.

One issue we went around and around about for years had to do with me wanting to return to college. I had completed two years before we married, and I wanted to finish my degree. When I'd mention wanting to go back to school, my husband would ask, "How are you going to pay for it? You would need to get a scholarship." I took his remarks to mean he didn't want me to go to school.

Looking back from the healthier place in which we are today, I have no idea why I interpreted his words that way. I suspect I was so afraid of not getting what I wanted, I preferred to think the worst and withdraw rather than face the issue, have an honest conversation, and overcome obstacles.

Bottom line, when one (or both!) partners withdraw from conflict, it's nearly impossible to land on a real solution that works for everyone.

18. Shutting Down

A friend of mine once described this behavior like this: "I felt so overwhelmed by not having an answer my spouse would validate, I would shut up and shut down. My words left me. He kept talking. I'd answer in my head, but not with my mouth because everything I said would be refuted, and I'd be made to look stupid. Whenever this happened, I literally could not think or come up with words to say. I'd emotionally freeze on the inside and say nothing."

I began to see this same behavior in myself. Instead of standing up for my preferences or beliefs—especially if the conversation became heated—I'd stop talking and become silent. This often occurred when I felt unheard and I assumed my response would not be validated.

Sometimes my husband would even think that we had come to an agreement on a topic, while I silently disagreed. I didn't think I could convince him of my perspective; therefore, I didn't even try.

Obviously, as you can see, I'm not shut down anymore!

19. Experiencing Chaos

Because there's such a drive to please everyone when you're stuck in a ditch, life gets chaotic. It's impossible to make everyone happy, but that didn't keep me from trying. I also tended to over-commit and say "yes" to too many things. This led to living in a rush, leaving important tasks unfinished, and getting behind on daily chores, which was a stressful way to live.

20. Playing the Victim

Though I never once voiced it this way, I felt like the victim. I felt wronged, walked on, ignored, disrespected, used, taken advantage of, and powerless to do anything about it. It's not that I always felt this way, but the victim card was one I definitely played in my head from time to time.

21. Wanting to Self-Harm

When feelings of powerlessness, anxiety, depression, or fear become overwhelming and all attempts to find relief fail, some people turn to self-harming behaviors. This could be passive or active.

Sometimes I'd engage in passive self-harming. I'd subconsciously go for the (slow) kill: eating too much, drinking too much, not exercising, playing solitaire till I could scream. Going into deprivation mode was another popular escape: *not* taking breaks, *not* eating, neglecting self-care, or depriving myself of my own needs. Reckless behavior such as driving too fast can be an act of passive self-harm as well.

More direct self-harming measures include cutting, picking at skin, pulling out hair, or engaging in other self-punishing acts. Self-harming behaviors lead down a dangerous and slippery slope and ultimately do not provide the relief we are seeking.

When hopelessness and powerlessness grow too large and overwhelming, tunnel vision and despair take over. The next step may be a suicide attempt. I came close to that once. Thanks to the friend who showed up, knocked at my door, and pulled me out of my abyss, I didn't go down that path.

Others aren't so lucky.

The twenty-one ditch behaviors explained above seem to be the most common; however, there are more. Check the Appendix to see an extensive, though not exhaustive, list.

When I finally realized I was stuck deep in what I came to understand as the "others-focused ditch," I wasn't too thrilled about my predicament. The first time I took inventory of my behaviors, I was shocked! I became aware for the first time that *every* one of those ways of acting were driven by fear and feeling powerless to do anything different. I had no idea how much fear affected my life!

The ditch was simply an extreme. I didn't know how to relate any other way, so I resorted to replicating the model with which I'd been raised. My actions were automatic, subconscious (or at best quasi-conscious), reactive, and pre-programmed. Until I awakened to the way I behaved, I was destined to continue defaulting to those methods. They were quite predictable, though I was oblivious to what I was doing.

See the others-focused chart on page 18.

AWARENESS: THE FIRST STEP TO CLIMBING OUT OF YOUR RUT

After taking inventory of my ditch and seeing how deep it was, I knew I was sick and tired of being mired down. I was fed up with feeling frustrated.

OTHERS
FOCUSED

ME
FOCUSED

Thoughts
Feelings
Concerns
Desires

1. People Pleaser
2. Default answer: yes
3. Readily give up what I want
4. Difficulty making decisions
5. Eggshells
6. Difficulty expressing
   thoughts/feelings
7. Avoiding
8. Co-dependent
9. Blaming
10. Passive
11. Obligated
12. Resentful
13. Sarcastic
14. Criticize/gossip
15. Hurt
16. Passive-Aggressive
17. Withdraw
18. Shut down
19. Chaotic
20. Victim
21. Self-harming

Subconscious
Automatic
Pre-Programmed
Reaction

Extreme
Powerless
Fear

Looking up from the bottom of my ditch, I took stock of my thought process. As I mentioned, for years I had focused only on what I thought my spouse wanted, desired, and felt. From my vantage point, he was focused on the same thing: what *he* was thinking, feeling, concerned about, and desiring.[1] Meanwhile, I wondered, who was thinking about me?

Well, no one was! Not even *me!*

As I began to admit that patterns of behaviors in my family had programmed me to value others and discount myself, I began to catch a glimpse of the solution to the problem.

I needed to start thinking of *me,* while at the same time remembering to take into consideration others' perspectives.

Truth be told, before becoming aware, I didn't even *know* how I felt. But once I began to acknowledge my emotions and finally identify what I was experiencing internally—I was able to admit to myself that fear and powerlessness were keeping me stuck!

My newfound awareness helped me find the path to crawling out of my ditch. The process was slow and tiring, but empowering and life-giving at the same time.

Once my eyes opened to my ditch dynamics, I grew curious about what else had been going on in my life that I had missed. And as I mustered the courage to peek out of my ditch, I began to learn things about my husband I'd never realized before.

POINTS TO PONDER:
- Ditches are extreme default behaviors
- They are subconscious, automatic, preprogrammed and reactionary
- They stem from fear and feeling powerless
- In the others-focused ditch our focus is on the other person's thoughts, feelings, concerns and desires
- Others-focused people tend to forget about their own needs and wants
- Climbing out of the ditch requires awareness and valuing both myself and others equally

CHAPTER 2

THE ME-FOCUSED DITCH

"Who looks outside, dreams; who looks inside, awakes."
—Carl Gustav Jung

From the time my husband and I started dating, I was convinced he wanted to control me. It seemed like his primary focus was on his own thoughts, feelings, concerns, and desires. I felt that he could be demanding. I didn't like that he would seem to get disappointed—and then angry—when I didn't live up to what he wanted.

Why did I put up with those behaviors? Well, even though I didn't like these patterns, they mirrored my life growing up. After all, my dad was like that, too. In my experience, men were simply more "me-focused." I thought that was just the way things were.

My husband and I married and, for the next thirty-five years, I tried to get him to change those things. I reasoned that if only he'd fix these four or five things, our life would be so much better.

I thought my problems were his fault; therefore, my hope for a better life rested solidly in his court. My focus was glued on his actions and what he needed to do differently. And it was true! If he *would* have changed those things, our lives *would* have been better! But he wasn't changing, and I felt stuck. Powerless. Frustrated.

However, the whole time I was frantically trying to improve him, I failed to see any issues with myself. For us to begin to heal and change, I needed to do more than recognize that dynamic—I would need to really own it.

Peering out from my ditch, I began to see that my husband's behavior was more predictable than I'd imagined. I also began to see the interplay between his default behaviors and my own. Finally, I was shocked to discover what was driving his behaviors!

21 "ME-FOCUSED" DEFAULT BEHAVIORS

While I was unconsciously defaulting to OF behaviors, my husband was unconsciously defaulting to "Me-Focused" (MF) behaviors.

(In this case, MF doesn't stand for what it means in the world of slang—although when we were both trapped in the worst of our mutual ditchy behaviors, I'd be lying if I said the thought never crossed my mind!)

You will hear more about the interplay between OF and MF couples' ditchy behaviors in following chapters, but first I want to describe 21 characteristics that are commonly attributed to people stuck in the rut on the MF side of the road:

1. Being Selfish

Spotting someone *else* being selfish is easy. You can easily see that *they* are thinking about what they want and disregarding what anyone else wants. My grandkids were over recently (ages five and three). We have two identical toy lawn mowers, except one is red and the other is green. You guessed it! My grandson wanted the red one already in use by his sister. He had no concern for what she might want. He just knew what he wanted. He tried taking it from her. She cried. Parents stepped in to make it right. But parents aren't there to intervene when you're thirty.

Kids grow up. The tendencies remain. We do the same thing in adulthood, though we are slightly more refined about it. Now, no one is around to help little Susie get her lawn mower back from her selfish boyfriend. Susie cries. She doesn't know what else to do. She's left frustrated and powerless. Meanwhile, both hold the illusion that the taker is in control. For the moment, perhaps that's true.

2. Defaulting to "No"

If a MF person gets asked to do something, go somewhere, or give permission, the default tendency is to automatically say "No." Later, the answer may shift from "no" to "maybe" or even "yes." But that's not usually the first answer they give.

A MF person tends to get into a relationship with an OF person who is inclined to automatically say "yes." It never occurred to me that my initial response could change, probably because once I said "yes," I usually followed through, even though I might regret or resent it. So, when my spouse responded with "no," I took that as his final answer, without clarifying, challenging, or directly asking him to consider my perspective.

3. Being a Perfectionist

According to the MF person's perspective, the goal is perfection. They learned to do it a certain way, and that's the way it needs to be done! OCD (obsessive compulsive disorder) fits in here, too.

MF people rarely stop to question why they think it needs to be done this way only. Others observe that it's "his way or the highway." This probably results from childhood, when harsh consequences may have followed not doing it "just right."

The MF individual has high standards for self and others. This is a good thing to a point. It's good to strive for excellence. However, because we are human, absolute perfection remains outside our ability to achieve. When we demand that of ourselves and others, contentment eludes us. The finished product invariably either ends up unfinished, or some minute flaw robs the crafter's ability to be pleased with the work. This leads to "next time I'll get it right" thinking. But next time comes with its own set of nicks and cracks. We look for perfect mates, too, with equally disappointing results.

4. Needing to be Right

MF people tend to think they are right. Probably because they often are. It's not wrong to be right. It's pride, gloating, attitude of superiority, or mocking of the person who didn't get it right that makes it ditchy. This "I'm right" stance affects the intimate partner in a couple of important ways. The partner learns to give up the fight most of the time. In addition, when partners attempt to win the game of "king of the facts," it ends up lose-lose and drives a wedge between the two.

For many years, my spouse and I were members of a church that believed and taught that we were the only true church, and every other church was wrong. As a member of that church, I adopted that belief as well. Without realizing it, we chose our stance of being "right" over relationships. We severed a lot of connections in the name of "the true church." Thankfully, the leadership discovered they weren't as "correct" as they thought they were. They had the strength of character to be humble enough to admit it to the entire organization and take steps to change. I, too, had to admit I was wrong. Through that, I learned: "We *all* see through a glass darkly" (1 Cor. 13:12 KJV).

When we are convinced we are right, we do not bother to look at the perspective of other people because we have already concluded they are wrong. That's why religion and politics create so many arguments. We often approach these topics with minds already made up, not open to seeing any other perspective.

5. Difficulty Seeing Other Perspectives

Speaking of perspective, MF partners have a hard time seeing a situation from any viewpoint other than their own. It's hard for them to put themselves in someone else's shoes.

That's why they sometimes appear to have the attitude that "it's my way or the highway." They truly can't see it any other way. Attempts by others to get them to see it differently fall on deaf ears.

A man I'll call George was in the hospital dying. His wife, who had medical power-of-attorney, was convinced her husband would not only survive, but be well enough to attend an upcoming party that was important to her. George suffered through treatments he didn't want, his arms filled with needles pumping fluids and a cocktail of medications through his veins. To prevent him from pulling out the needles and his oxygen mask, his arms were strapped to the bed. For several days, he'd been forced to lay in that position.

He mentioned to his son that this was "torture" and he didn't want to be there anymore. Nevertheless, his MF wife was adamant about him being at that celebration and had the legal power to make the medical decisions. She could not empathize with his predicament; her own desires for him to attend the party blinded her to what he wanted and needed.

6. Demanding

Continuing with the example of the spat between the grandkids, my grandson then came to me, demanding that I let him have the coveted red lawn mower. Those kinds of demands work with about 50 percent of the population (who are OF people) because they've been programmed to readily give up what they want. But it doesn't always work. It's ineffective with other MF. When one MF person makes demands of another MF person, the result is typically an argument. Because it usually works with OFs, it can become a favorite go-to behavior of the MF person.

7. Manipulating

If my husband wanted something, he'd make suggestions, knowing I'd jump to do what he wanted. It seemed he could easily talk me *out* of doing something I wanted that he didn't want, or *into* something he wanted that I didn't. He would pout, shoulders slumped forward in disappointment, or utter some remark to convince me to cave in to his wishes. I definitely felt manipulated!

Another form of manipulation happens when comments are intended to spur feelings of guilt. Driven by that guilt, I'd do what he wanted. He'd bring up something or say it in such a way that I felt bad if I didn't go along with his proposed course of action.

This echoed manipulative comments my parents had made to get me to do what they wanted. "You'd better clean up your plate because of all the starving children in China." As an adult, my ability to catch faulty logic did not improve. No options other than to comply or risk further punishment appeared to exist.

8. Being Critical

As I mentioned, I grew up with critical parents, especially my dad. The words "Can't you do anything right?" reverberated in my head as a result of hearing it so often as a child. I felt criticized by my spouse too. He'd complain to me about all kinds of things that I didn't do right. Even when he didn't make overt comments, it was easy for me to feel criticized. Yes, he was generous with his disapproval, but I was also overly sensitive to disapproval. It was a devastating combination.

9. Controlling

We already discussed how I felt controlled. Not feeling free to do what I wanted, I blamed my husband for controlling me. He'd frequently say "no" to requests I made. It seemed that we only went to movies when it was something he wanted to see.

Statements that tell others what to do or not do feel controlling to the recipient. Examples include: "You don't want to do that." "Why would you want to go?" "You can't do anything anyway." "Don't talk to men. I don't talk to other women."

I tended to use a more indirect approach: "Do you want to go to a movie?"

His response: "No, I don't want to go."

Since his automatic first response to anything tended to be "no," I adopted the belief that he didn't want to do anything I wanted.

If I really wanted to go, I'd come back with, "I heard it got rave reviews, and Fran said we should see it," adding information in hopes that would sway his decision. (Without realizing it, I was manipulating instead of being forthright.)

He'd retort, "Why do you always challenge what I say?" That added further to my fear of speaking up and asking for what I wanted.

Never once did it occur to me to consider changing how I approached the subject. Feeling defeated, I'd be upset at him for not taking me into consideration, and we would end up not going to the movie.

His method of evaluation seemed to go like this: *Do I want to go to a movie? Yes? No? No, I don't want to go.* To me it seemed that he considered only his own thoughts, feelings, concerns, and desires in the process. It never dawned on me that his method of deciding was different than my approach. Do you remember what my thought process was? Refer to Chapter 1 to review. Comparing the ditchy differences can be enlightening. We both learned unhealthy ways of relating and didn't know any better.

10. Being Vocal About Feelings and Wants

My husband tends to be outspoken about what he wants and needs. He's straightforward about his likes and dislikes. When he's upset with me, he lets me know. I'm not left guessing. In a healthy relationship, that's good. In an unhealthy relationship, it fed into my belief that my thoughts and feelings didn't matter.

Often, the mode of delivery, tone of voice, expression, and volume becomes the ditchy part. Also, subtleties of word choice make it hard for the OF to speak up. The MF wants their own way, and the OF tends to comply. Both are programmed to see it the way they do. Both believe the MF's opinion matters more.

My default pattern led me to hold thoughts in, while he tended to be vocal. His outspokenness added to my belief that I needed to suppress how I felt and comply with what he wanted. Neither of us were conscious of our templates.

11. Having High Expectations

My husband expected many things from me. He expected me to clean the house, do the dishes, cook, attend to the laundry, shop, take care of the kids, and help with income. After all, that's what he witnessed his mom doing. His dad worked, gardened, read the paper, and watched TV, while his mom took care of everything else and waited on his dad hand and foot. My spouse grew up expecting his wife to be like the model he witnessed from his parents and subconsciously expected that his life would mirror his dad's. Of course, my parents provided a similar example.

Which is why, for over thirty-five years of my marriage, if coffee got served, the waitress was me.

But the biggest expectation centered around being "on time." It didn't matter if we were headed to a social event, a business meeting, or church, we *had* to arrive early. My partner would be upset if we were even a few minutes late according to the time he predetermined we should arrive. The pattern tended to look like this: I'd get out of the house on time, only to remember that I'd forgotten a necessary item, which then I had to run back in to retrieve. That made me late. Often the conversation the entire way to the event focused on my tardiness and how upsetting that was to him. No matter how hard I tried, something always seemed to get in the way of me meeting his timeliness expectations. Afraid to be late, I'd rush out, which perpetuated the problem, because in a hurry, I forgot things.

12. Feeling Disappointed

On the heels of high expectations, disappointment often follows. In other words, we have a goal we would like to see happen. At the same time, subconsciously, we believe the other person isn't going to live up to what we want. When the expectation does not get met, it proves that, once again, we're "right." We then feel justified in being upset about it.

Yet this pattern of high expectations combined with anticipated failure and "justified" disappointment sets up the other person to disappoint us.

13. Being Angry

This high bar of perfectionism combined with expectations and disappointments causes the MF a lot of built-up anger fueled by fear of not getting the desired results. It's frustrating when people don't do what the MF wants done. Furthermore, because of failed attempts, the intensity of negative emotion increases.

Unresolved anger builds up and leaks out on the people nearby. Road rage is a great example of misplaced anger. Another driver commits a minor infraction, maybe driving too close or cutting in front, which sparks a powder keg for the person already furious about other things in life. Last week, my husband witnessed a driver slipping in front of someone just before stopping at a red light. The person who got cut off pulled a gun on the man in front of him! Luckily, no shots got fired. The infraction did not warrant the reaction!

At a more personal level, spouses and kids may suffer the brunt of a family member's fury, even though the real source driving the emotion came from something that may have happened earlier in the day, last week, or even during childhood! Anytime my husband seemed angry, I simply couldn't distinguish the legitimate source or object of his frustration I always assumed the anger was directed at me and never thought to ask or question the true source of his temper. I reacted by becoming a master feather-smoother. I worked hard at trying to please him, attempting to keep his anger at bay and straighten his ruffled feathers.

14. Demeaning

In certain situations, a MF may resort to demeaning the other person in the form of mocking, pointing out flaws, and put downs. It's an attempt to deflect from hidden internal feelings of inadequacy or frustration we often don't even realize exists. We got demeaned during childhood, so when our children behave in similar ways to how we did, we pass on the same reaction we got from our parents.

Examples of demeaning comments include: "I thought you could do better than that. I guess I was wrong." "You're good for nothing." "You're lazy." Usually, there's a mocking or "I'm better than you" tone that goes along with it.

15. Threatening

Many people grew up with parents who used verbal threats, shaming, or guilting, to gain compliance. Threats can also include physical punishment, loss of privileges or belongings. I'm talking about extremes here, not consequences that are established intentionally to build character. We'll look at the balance when we talk about road behaviors.

In a romantic relationship, threats can include frequent promises to end the relationship if a partner doesn't do something or other. (I'm not saying there's never a time to talk about breaking up, and I'll talk about appropriate times and ways to end a relationship in Chapter 7). But a ditchy threat has frightening undertones. It may manifest as intent to do bodily harm, destroy property, deprive or hurt emotionally. It is a method used to coerce someone into compliance. Ditchy threats may also involve some form of public shaming. Blackmail fits in here. Often, because of fear of consequences or memory of past experiences when threats were carried out, the victim cowers and complies. Threats scare a person into conforming.

Unhealthy threats include comments such as: "I'll post that incriminating picture of you on Facebook!" "I'll break your favorite vase!" "I'm telling [someone you don't want to know] what you did." "You'll be sorry!" "I'm going to hurt [someone you care about] or destroy [something of yours] if you don't do what I want."

16. Yelling

My parents yelled at us when we didn't do what they wanted. I yelled at my kids too. When we get angry, it's a natural reaction to raise our voices, use a more forceful tone, or speak through clenched teeth. It's so common we don't even think of it as a ditchy thing to do. It seems normal and natural. It *is normal.* It's just not healthy or godly. It's an attempt to regain control when we feel like we've lost control.

17. Attacking/Accusing

Though attacking is synonymous with aggressive actions, I'm referring here to any behavior that causes the other person to react in a defensive way. This may sound odd, but when we accuse the other person of being defensive, that, too, is an attack! That doesn't diminish the fact that the accusation may be 100 percent true.

Examples of a verbal attacks include statements that label, blame, accuse, or criticize another. "You are lazy." "It's your fault we're late." "You lied to me." "You did this wrong." "Why don't you ever do anything right?" "You said you'd do that, but you didn't." "Why don't you ever bring me flowers?" "You'll never amount to anything." "You don't think!"

Some of those comments were normal in my house growing up. What were some common phrases used in your house? Even if some of these things are true, the way they are stated may cause the other person to feel attacked, and comments like this erode self-esteem.

Attacks take a lot of forms: an angry look, shaking a finger, a raised voice, accusing, blocking exits, and breaking or throwing things. Forcefully placing your hands on your hips with a stern look on your face and anger shooting from your eyes illustrates a mild form of an attack.

When we grow up in homes where we see this kind of behavior modeled, frequently we end up copying it or getting into a relationship where it is perpetuated. We don't want to be in a relationship like that but have no way of knowing how to avoid it. We block out how traumatized we were by what we witnessed and unwittingly repeat the pattern unless we become aware of how life can be different and work on healing from our childhood wounds. Whether we become the victim or aggressor, we replicate what we learned; therefore, we must change our own ways of relating.

Some people make conscious decisions not to treat their children the way they were treated by their parents—and then go to the opposite extreme of becoming too lenient, in which case the other parent may become the overbearing one. I became too permissive in some areas because I didn't want to act the way my parents did but didn't know what to do instead. This created space for my husband to compensate for my lack by become overbearing at times with our children.

18. Being Rigid

In this extreme, we find rigid adherence to rules, and an obsessive compulsive need to do things in a certain way or manifest narrow and restricted ways of acting. Rigidity provides an illusion of protection and safety because following rules makes us feel "safe."

19. Being Addicted

To self-medicate all the pain, anger, disappointment, and rage that builds up inside, MF people may tend to turn to some form of addiction to soothe or distract. An addiction is simply a manner of coping with the intolerable, for someone who does not know any other method of escape. Two of our most common ways of self-soothing are through food and sex. It's not surprising that eating disorders and sexual issues abound. Even seemingly innocuous activities—housekeeping, working, exercising, playing on our phones, scrolling through Facebook—can become an addiction if it helps us avoid our deep emotional pain.

20. Physical Attacks

Deep in the MF ditch, aggressive behavior—throwing things, punching, hitting, slapping, biting, hair pulling—can result in physical harm. Frustration runs at an all-time high, and the intense feeling of powerlessness and anger at the other person drives this aggressive behavior. At this point, the individual is in complete react mode, losing control of their actions.

21. Harming Others

In extreme situations, this results in destruction of property, harming animals, and injuring or killing others. People with intense rage turn into perpetrators of abuse and crime. If you'd like some examples, watch the nightly news.

THE TRUTH I DIDN'T SEE COMING

For most of my life, I was convinced that MF behaviors were the worst. After all, the me-focused default gets stuck on "*my* thoughts, *my* feelings, *my* concerns, and *my* desires" to the exclusion of the other person. In this mode, they forget to consider what anyone else thinks, feels, fears, or wants.

From my victim viewpoint, I smugly told myself, *I'd never even THINK of doing those things.*

Because I also felt controlled by me-focused people, I believed they were in control. I thought people in the other ditch had all the power because I didn't have any. I certainly *felt* controlled.

Imagine my surprise when I discovered that MF's also sometimes *feel trapped, powerless and driven by fear!* They learned to be controlling because, at some point in childhood, life fell apart when they were helpless to do anything about it. They attempt to control the environment around them because of internal feelings of powerlessness and not being in control of their own emotions.

I eventually realized that MF behaviors are not rooted in arrogance but in fear. They are not driven by power, but by powerlessness.

The truth is that the efforts of MF people to control others are simply attempts to make their own world feel comfortable and safe. My spouse and I both lived unaware of the cause of our underlying relationship struggles. All he knew was that the world felt safer for him when he was in control of situations and the actions of others, which provided an illusion of power and safety. All was fine, as long as others complied.

However, controlling others or external circumstances fails to bring peace to the MF's internal world and is just as futile as an OF's attempts to gain love and acceptance by giving up control and people pleasing.

In other words, behaviors from *both* ditches are driven by fear, and behaviors from *both* ditches disempower, cause frustration, and prove ineffective in the long run.

Every ditch behavior stems from an attempt to navigate our world in the best way possible. We work hard at it, but behaviors coming from the ditch ultimately prove ineffective. They only add to the frustration we already experience. They cause distancing instead of the closeness we desire and strive to achieve.

Just as OF people get stuck replicating the model they experienced growing up, MF people do the same thing. Their actions are automatic, subconscious (or at best quasi-conscious), reactive, and pre-programmed.

Below is what MF ditch behaviors look like:

**ME
FOCUSED**

Thoughts
Feelings
Concerns
Desires

Subconscious
Automatic
Pre-Programmed
Reaction

1. Selfish
2. Default answer: no
3. Perfectionism
4. I'm right
5. Difficulty seeing other perspective
6. Demanding
7. Manipulative
8. Critical
9. Controlling
10. Vocal about feelings
11. Expectations
12. Disappointment
13. Angry
14. Demeaning
15. Threatening
16. Yelling
17. Attacking/Accusing
18. Rigid
19. Addicted
20. Physical Attacks
21. Harming Others

Extreme
Powerless
Fear

If you're thinking it doesn't paint such a pretty picture, neither ditch does. That's why it's a ditch! Lots of junk accumulates on both sides. After all, think about what can collect in any ditch on the side of a road: water, mud, weeds, trash, bottles, bugs, and snakes.

I tried for over thirty-five years to get my husband to come out of his ditch. It was so much easier to see his ditchy doings than it was to see my own. Remember, I was focused on him to the exclusion of me for most of my life. I was blind to what I could do differently, but I sure had opinions on what *he* ought to change and tried to convince him in every ditchy way I knew! I begged and cajoled. I tried to pull him out of his ditch. I climbed into his ditch and tried to push him out.

But nothing worked until I was willing to realize I lived in my own ditch, too. Healing evaded us until I began focusing on my own predicament instead of his.

WE DON'T HAVE TO KEEP REPEATING THE PAST

Not everyone is guilty of every type of behavior listed in the two ditches. We all have our go-to favorites and there are some behaviors we have never embraced. I'm not saying that because an individual identifies with one ditch or the other that it means they will end up resorting to serious self-harm, suicide, harming others, or criminal activity. Those behaviors are severe, and most of us don't even come close to falling that deep into the ravine. But I believe we can't ignore where the progression of extremes— driven by fear and feeling powerless—can lead if we continue unaware.

It's particularly critical for people—either OF or MF—who come from homes where their caregivers tended toward abusive behavior to recognize the fears driving their reactions and learn how to combat them.

The good news is that by recognizing our own reactions and naming the fears that ignite them, a pathway out of the mire emerges.

There is hope. Healing is not just a far-fetched idea. It is very much within your grasp.

POINTS TO PONDER:

- Both ditches are filled with default behaviors acquired during childhood.
- Me-Focused people tend to consider only their own thoughts, feelings, concerns and desires.
- They get stuck in an extreme where they also feel powerless and behaviors are driven by fear.
- Ditches are our best attempt to navigate because we don't know any other way.
- Ditch behaviors create distance instead of the closeness we desire.
- The pathway out of the ditch involves considering others and valuing their perspectives equally with one's own views.

CHAPTER 3

WHAT DRIVES DITCH BEHAVIORS

"Fear Is a Liar."
—*Zach Williams*

For most of my life I had no idea I felt afraid, nor did I see myself as powerless. Most of the time, fear ran under the radar, and I didn't recognize it as such. It masqueraded behind anger, hurt, anxiety, depression, frustration, inferiority, insecurity, trauma, sadness, stress, shame, and guilt. There may be other places it hides, too, but those are the most common.

Before I became aware of what was happening inside me emotionally, if asked, I would have described it this way: "inside seems black." Well, "black" is not a feeling! It never occurred to me to identify or get in touch with my inner psyche to describe my experience. That's the stealth of fear. It's disguised so well that I didn't pick up on it. I was trapped into repeating the same old ineffective habits, hoping that *this time* results would be different. And, of course, because I did the same things, I got the same results. I didn't know any other way.

The ditches represent default behaviors which are preprogrammed, automatic, subconscious, and reactive. When we dip beneath the surface of the road, we enter into the realm of fear, the driving force behind every ditch reaction. It's like entering foggy, gray-brown, murky water where it's impossible to see clearly what's happening. Awareness of why we do what we do when in the ditch, the effects those behaviors have on others and on us, and the consequences of those actions escape our attention. On top of that, we keep repeating the same thing throughout our lives until we become aware and begin to change. It's like we're under a spell. And, indeed we are! Some people never gain the awareness they so desperately need. *We* can see they need it, but they can't. And conversely, they are aware of our need to change when we are blind to it.

Fear drives all those ditchy behaviors. That's the hex that has hypnotized us. We are told "God has not given us the spirit of fear; but of power, and of love, and of a sound mind" (2 Tim. 1:7, KJV). It took me forever to understand this verse. It says, "spirit of fear." When in the ditch, I failed to pick up on the fact that *fear is a spirit!* So that hazy murkiness enveloping me consisted of a fear spirit! No wonder I couldn't see! Fear blinded me!

Let's look at the ways fear can be described. The online thesaurus offers these options: "angst, anxiety, concern, despair, dismay, doubt, dread, horror, jitters, panic, scare, suspicion, terror, unease, uneasiness, worry, abhorrence, agitation, aversion, awe, consternation, cowardice, creeps, discomposure, disquietude, distress, faintheartedness, foreboding, fright, funk, misgiving, nightmare, phobia, presentiment, qualm, reverence, revulsion, timidity, trembling, tremor, trepidation, bête noire, chicken heartedness, cold feet, cold sweat, recreancy."[1] In addition, the following words come to mind: nervous, afraid, apprehension, tension, stress, strain, terrified, frightened. And there are more ways to describe the dark spirits that plague us. We are driven to our ditches when these fears come knocking and we don't recognize their influence. Therefore, we react instead of responding.

Following, you will find possible fears driving ditch behaviors. However, there may be other culprits. A brief illustration is provided in conjunction with each ditchy action, but there may be many more.

Fears Driving Others-Focused Behaviors:
- **People Pleasing**: Fear of the disapproval of others.
- **Default Answer "Yes"**: Fear of displeasing or disappointing others.
- **Readily Giving up What I Want**: Fear of rejection if I hold to my desires.
- **Difficulty Making Decisions**: Fear of making the wrong decision or upsetting others with my decision.
- **Walking on Eggshells**: Fear of saying or doing something that will cause the other person to be upset.
- **Difficulty Expressing Feelings or Opinions**: Fear of my feelings being invalidated, discounted, or denied.
- **Avoiding:** Fear of getting into an argument I can't win.
- **Co-dependence**: Fear of the other person's reaction or anger.
- **Blaming**: Fear of not being able to do anything about it. (Belief that it's the other person's fault and waiting for them to fix it.)
- **Being Passive:** Fear of standing up for self; fear of conflict.
- **Feeling Obligated:** Fear of having no choice; fear it won't get done if I don't do it.

- **Being Resentful**: Fear of not mattering or not being important.
- **Being Sarcastic**: Fear of a negative reaction if I express my true feelings.
- **Being Critical and/or Gossipy**: Fear of confronting the person causing the problem.
- **Nursing Hurts**: Fear that if feelings were expressed, they would not be validated.
- **Being Passive-Aggressive**: Fear of retaliation if feelings were expressed directly.
- **Withdrawing:** Fear of being unheard or not valued; fear of conflict.
- **Shutting down**: Fear of making any move at all, or fear of retaliation if a move is made.
- **Experiencing Chaos:** Fear of being rejected if everyone is not pleased.
- **Playing the Victim**: Fear of not having an advocate; fear it will always be this way.
- **Wanting to Self-Harm**: Fear that circumstances will never improve; fear of being unlovable or unacceptable.

Fears Driving Me-Focused Behaviors:
- **Selfish:** Fear of not getting what is needed.
- **Default Answer "No"**: Fear of making a wrong decision.
- **Perfectionist:** Fear of not being loved or accepted.
- **Need to be Right**: Fear of judgment or condemnation; fear of being wrong.
- **Difficulty Seeing Other Perspectives:** Fear of not getting desires met.
- **Demanding:** Fear of not being obeyed.

- **Manipulating:** Fear others won't agree to one's direct wishes.
- **Critical:** Deflecting from fear of inadequacy by pointing out the flaws of others.
- **Controlling:** Fear of bad things happening when others are in control.
- **Vocal about Feelings and Wants:** Fear of being pushed aside.
- **High Expectations:** Fear people will not live up to those standards.
- **Disappointment:** Fear of not getting desires met.
- **Angry:** Fear of abandonment, of not being loved or accepted; fear the wrong won't be made right.
- **Demeaning:** Fear of hurt and vulnerability.
- **Threatening:** Fear others won't comply.
- **Yelling:** Fear of losing control.
- **Attacking/Accusing:** Fear that no one else will protect me.
- **Rigid:** Fear of consequences or fear of chaos if rules aren't followed.
- **Addict:** Fear of being stuck in the situation forever.
- **Physical attacks:** Fear of being harmed or humiliated.
- **Harming Others:** Fear of intense internal powerlessness; fear of having no control.

Other possible fears or feelings may be at the bottom of your ditchy actions. Hopefully this is enough to get you pondering what drives those go-to reactions. Sometimes our emotions are hidden from our own awareness, and it may take some digging to discover exactly which fears drive the bus.

WHO FALLS INTO DITCHES?

Ditches are not gender specific, though you may tend to find more men in the me-focused ditch and more women in the others-focused ditch. It makes sense when you think about the roles men and women are expected to play in American culture. Men traditionally worked as breadwinners, women as homemakers and nurturers. Men were served; women were acculturated to serve. This pattern is shifting, resulting in more men identifying as OFs and more women as MFs. Who knows? It might fit the arbitrary 80/20 rule.

In recovery circles, the OF may be labeled "co-dependent," "victim," or "suicidal." Common labels MFs get stuck with include "narcissistic," "addict," or "perpetrator." Those labels carry a lot of shame for the struggling individual. Truth be told, we all do ditchy things; it's just a matter of degree. While I've never killed a person, I've certainly harbored hatred in my heart, and God puts them both on the same plane just as He does lust and adultery (Matt. 5:28 KJV).

As humans, we categorize mistakes. Some we consider worse than others. We rank transgressions from minor to major, but in God's eyes all sin is the same, regardless of how small or great. To God, telling a white lie is as bad as murder. This concept challenges our beliefs because we rank and compare our shortcomings with those whose actions we deem worse. God does not do that. If you are hanging over a cliff holding onto a chain, each link labeled with a different sin, does it matter if you break the "murder," "gossip," or "lie" link? Only one connection needs to break for the hapless individual to end up at the bottom of the canyon. Categorization and comparison provide a false sense of superiority, where we consider ourselves better than others "because I don't do *that*," whatever we have determined "that" to be.

Our negative pre-programming shows up in ditch behaviors because they are subconscious, automatic, and reactive. We resort to them without thinking. We are oblivious of the effects and consequences in our lives and the lives of others. When someone is in the me-focused ditch, it's impossible to see through the dirt to really see what's going on with the other person.

And when I am in the others-focused ditch, I can't see clearly either. Who can't I see when I'm in the others-focused ditch? Myself! When I'm in that OFful (awful) ditch, my binoculars are fixed on my spouse and what I believe he is thinking, feeling, or desiring.[2] It doesn't matter if what I believe is true or not. The story I've made up in my head about what he's thinking is the one I'm convinced is true. Meanwhile, I ignore my own pleading: *What about me and what I want?* I turn a deaf ear to myself.

Pictured below are the OF and MF ditches, full of ditch behaviors on either side of the road. The actions don't necessarily correlate directly, but they may. For example, "people pleaser" is not the opposite of "selfish." Neither are they in a set order.

Remember, the driving force of every ditchy behavior is fear of *something*.

SO HOW DO WE END UP IN THE DITCH WE'RE IN?

Many of us were born in ditches.

Our childhoods play an indisputable role because we tend to perpetuate the actions we saw modeled growing up, especially when one parent tended to be others-focused, and the other me-focused. When this is the case, we typically grow up identifying with one parent, becoming like that parent, and adopting the same OF or MF ditchy behaviors we witnessed throughout our childhood.

OTHERS FOCUSED   # ME FOCUSED

Thoughts
Feelings
Concerns
Desires

OTHERS FOCUSED	Subconscious Automatic Pre-Programmed Reaction	ME FOCUSED
1. People Pleaser		1. Selfish
2. Default answer: yes		2. Default answer: no
3. Readily give up what I want		3. Perfectionism
4. Difficulty making decisions		4. I'm right
5. Eggshells		5. Difficulty seeing other
6. Difficulty expressing thoughts/feelings		perspective
7. Avoiding		6. Demanding
8. Co-dependent		7. Manipulative
9. Blaming		8. Critical
10. Passive		9. Controlling
11. Obligated		10. Vocal about feelings
12. Resentful		11. Expectations
13. Sarcastic		12. Disappointment
14. Criticize/gossip		13. Angry
15. Hurt		14. Demeaning
16. Passive-Aggressive		15. Threatening
17. Withdraw		16. Yelling
18. Shut down		17. Attacking/accusing
19. Chaotic		18. Rigid
20. Victim		19. Addicted
21. Self-harming		20. Physical Attacks
		21. Harming others

Extreme   Extreme
Powerless   Powerless
Fear   Fear
Greatest fear: rejection   Greatest fear: abandonment
Tendency: to abandon   Tendency: to reject
Difficult to admit: I allowed that   Difficult to admit: I did that

Then, as adults, we pull into our lives a love interest who at some level echoes the ditchy ways of the other parent.

This doesn't happen always, but it happens more often than we'd like to believe. We aren't carbon copies of our parents. There are just enough differences that the similarities may be difficult to recognize.

I've already confessed that the OF ditch was my ditch. You may have heard of "drug of choice." Well, that was my ditch of choice (DOC), acquired by observing my parents and emulating my mom's pattern, for the most part.

If we're honest, we'll admit that families can be pretty jacked up. During my childhood, my siblings and I helped Dad on the farm with crops and animals, and it didn't take much to cause him to yell at us. Not understanding what he wanted from us could spark an angry outburst. He'd ask for a tool and if I said, "Which one?" he'd raise his voice, point towards the full toolbox, and yell, "That one!" (as if the issue was my inability to hear and speaking in a louder tone would solve the problem!). Thankfully, he mostly just yelled, and I only remember him getting out the strap a few times.

My point is that, all too often, yelling, fighting, abuse, and neglect occur within the four walls of the dwelling supposed to be synonymous with "safe" and "peaceful." For millions, home turns out to be anything but that, and sometimes can feel like the most dangerous place to be.

For that matter, even well-intentioned parents can contribute to a child feeling rejected. When an overwhelmed parent tells a whining child to "go away" or ignores the child, it may be interpreted as rejection, which is not what the parent intended at all!

Many circumstances can lead to a child feeling rejected, such as getting picked on at school or having mean siblings or neighbors. Children can be told by people other than their parents that they are unloved or unwanted, or subjected to actions that send the message that no one wants or loves them. Teachers, clergy, friends, and neighbors may be unintentionally or purposefully rejecting.

For some children, home might feel safe but life does not. A war breaks out. 9/11 happens. A natural disaster occurs. The breadwinner loses a job. A parent gets sick. Someone dies. Through no fault of the parents, kids fall into a ditch because of trauma in life. Whether the child becomes others- or me-focused depends on the circumstances and the role the child plays in the family.

For example, my hemophiliac brother was born when I was two years old. His blood didn't clot, so countless hours were spent caring for him when he had internal or external bleeds. My parents *had* to take care of him, or he could die. When both he and I needed attention at the same time, my brother's needs trumped mine. Kids pick up on that dynamic quickly. I felt unloved, though it was no direct fault of my parents. Plus, I had an older sister who felt pushed aside when I was born, and she took it out on me, so I felt rejected by her too. My default path became others focused, because at least I got some attention for helping.

The fear of rejection terrifies an OF. Somewhere along the line, OF people typically have experienced rejection, or maybe inherited the feeling. To protect from that pain, we subconsciously conclude that the secret to love and acceptance is in people-pleasing and trying to make others happy by giving up one's own desires. Sadly, we fail to catch on that it doesn't really work in the long haul. We're left feeling taken advantage of, unloved, unaccepted—*and* we didn't get what we really wanted either!

By the way, when an OF person anticipates rejection, the automatic reaction is to abandon the relationship before getting pushed away. Subconscious logic: *"It's less painful if I leave. That way, I maintain the illusion that it was my choice, and I had control.* The OF may even fantasize that the person they abandoned is waiting patiently for their return, when there will be a joyous reunion, and all will magically be perfect. Because it is a self-protective ditch maneuver, the abandoner remains unaware of the hurt he or she caused by leaving, nor is the person conscious of the fear of rejection driving the behavior. The severed relationship never gets discussed. The one who got left behind is mystified about what happened. The latest term for this is "ghosting," when a person disappears from a relationship without explanation. I have been guilty of that. And now that I'm aware, I'm very sorry! This is a public apology to every person I've ever ditched with no explanation. For years, I truly didn't know what drove my behavior. Cluelessness keeps OFs from seeing the impact of their actions on others.

People land in the me-focused ditch because, at some level, their physical or emotional needs or wants were unmet. Children who struggle with abandonment issues may have lost a parent. Many other circumstances can also foster that gut-wrenching feeling of being left alone, along with fear of it happening again: parents caring for their elderly parents, a parent in the military, traveling for work, or going through a divorce are some of the most common reasons. Even if both parents are around, one or both may have "checked out" emotionally or be ill, addicted, or otherwise disconnected from their kids. Parents who have lost a close loved one to death may get caught up in their own grief, rendering them incapable of fully tending to the needs of their children.

Those kids had to grow up fast and take care of themselves, often becoming responsible for younger family members as well. Children who become caregivers for their parent or siblings miss out on receiving the care they need because of the role reversal. In the case of terminally ill parents, chronic pain, and many other circumstances, it's unavoidable! No wonder they became me-focused! A child doesn't realize it but feels deeply wounded for not getting the needed attention. This fosters resentment, and, unbeknownst to them, that anger leaks out in their everyday life, especially on the closest family members, who were not the cause of their initial anger, but inadvertently do things that spark an angry reaction. Spouses and children interpret the anger as being directed at them, when most of the time it's simply a current incident triggering an old, dry, powder keg of a memory. MFs search for someone who will finally give them the care they needed but didn't get, which explains their attraction to OFs.

I mentioned that my sister felt pushed aside when I came along, and then we had a brother who required a lot of attention for medical reasons. She felt abandoned. As the oldest child, she had to fend for herself and became responsible for more at a younger age, so she landed in the MF ditch, whereas I landed in the OF ditch.

Sometimes it's easier to look at family members and see what they exhibit than it is to see our own behaviors. Start your awareness journey by noticing how people manifest ditchy behaviors in TV shows and movies. The MF and OF patterns became clearer to me as I considered my other family members. From my family of origin, two of us landed in the OF and two in the MF ditch. The role each of us played in the family, birth order, illnesses, and more influenced our DOC (Ditches of Choice). My dad was an MF and my mom was an OF. I became an OF and married a MF.

Which ditch characteristics best match your mom and dad? Stepparents? Grandparents? Siblings? You may notice that your siblings populate both ditches: some are on one side; the rest are on the other.

To recap, we land in ditches when we're born into a severely dysfunctional family, get pushed in because of circumstances, or fall in because of an event that happens while we're growing up. Once we're adults, we have become so accustomed to our ditch behaviors that we run to them when we don't know what else to do. We pull out our favorite reactions and hurl them at the other from the safety of the weeds we're hiding behind in our ditch.

STUDYING THE PAST CAN BE A CATALYST FOR CHANGE, HEALING, FORGIVENESS

In one of my classes during graduate school an assignment required an interview with an octogenarian. My mom had passed away by then, and at age 80, my dad was in the required age group, so I decided to interview him. I learned a lot about his childhood that I had never thought to ask him about before, and by the end of our conversation I understood how several key factors played a major role in *his* life and contributed to the development of *his* reactionary pattern. Today, people would say he suffered from post-traumatic stress disorder (PTSD).

First, my dad's father became ill with edema when my dad was a teenager and eventually died at age 59. My grandpa couldn't work, leaving my dad responsible for the farm at the tender age of 13. At the time of the interview with my dad, my youngest son had just become a teenager. I pictured my son saddled with such responsibility and could only imagine how overwhelmed and alone my father must have felt!

Secondly, Dad served as a medic during World War II on the front lines in Europe. In a matter-of-fact tone he told me, "One time, a shell exploded next to my Red Cross ambulance, and I saw an angel on the hood. My teammate didn't survive, but I was spared." He also talked about his battalion freeing the

Mauthausen-Gusen concentration camp complex. He spoke like it was yesterday's news, completely devoid of any emotional connection. When I saw movie clips of Mauthausen's liberation on the Internet a few years after he died, I finally understood at a deeper level why his only comment about it was, "Some of them were just too far gone to save." Disconnecting feelings from the horrors he witnessed was the only way he could still function. Understandably, I also think he experienced survivor guilt for not being able to save some of the men under his care. So, like many other good soldiers, he unplugged himself from his experience. In so doing, he flatlined his emotions.

After surviving WWII, Dad married my mother, and they had five children. Two were born with hemophilia, a genetic condition in which blood doesn't clot. My dad worked full time in a factory, which provided our family with good health insurance, only to come home to his second full-time job as a farmer. He was chronically deprived of sleep because of the unrelenting work staring him in the face, not to mention that he worked the swing shift. That meant his work schedule rotated every two weeks from days, to afternoons, to midnights. No wonder he often fell asleep at the table! His biological clock was always screwed up! That kind of schedule would make anyone irritable and short-fused. Sadly, his annual month off from the factory was spent working on the farm. As a farmer, factory worker, and father, he never got any real vacation or rest.

Growing up, my dad never talked about how he felt about any of that. Life was lived, not discussed. Conversations centered around facts, events, what someone else did, or who died. Discussions revolved around what needed to be done, not feelings or opinions. Until my dad died, a typical exchange on the phone with him went something like this: "What's the price of gas there in Colorado?" His other main topic concerned what food needed to be used up in the refrigerator before it spoiled. Those topics were "safe." They didn't involve emotions.

My mom, on the other hand, was passive and emotionally shut down, too, but in a quiet way. She tried her darnedest to keep peace to avoid triggering angry outbursts from my dad. My grandma, whom I adored, lived up the road a quarter mile on the family homestead where the barn, machinery, and most of the cattle resided. That was the main farming operation, but we also had a barn and fields where we lived, too, so Dad went back and forth between the two places daily. I remember Mom would be working at the kitchen sink and see dad coming down the road on the tractor, so she'd drop what she was doing to go open the gate for dad so he wouldn't have to get off the tractor—as if what she was doing didn't matter. I think maybe she did that to keep his fuse from getting lit. It also illustrates how she valued what *he* wanted or needed above her own work. I believe Mom also genuinely wanted to please him and felt that much could be gained by making my dad happy.

My mother grew up with five younger brothers. As the oldest and only girl, helping with taking care of her younger siblings, cooking, cleaning, and anything else considered "woman's work" fell on her shoulders. In her era, boys weren't expected or asked to do that kind of work. Unfortunately, that same mindset got passed down to my generation. After all of us spent the day working in the hay or doing other farm work, my sister and I still had to help with dinner and dishes while our brothers got to sit and watch TV. We frequently complained, to no avail, "Why don't the boys have to help with the dishes?"

For a few years as a teenager, I wished I was a boy. I even wrote an English paper about it once, not because of any confusion in my sexual identity; I just wanted the same privileges my brothers got. The inequality of value assigned to men's and women's roles contributed to my feelings of inadequacy, dissatisfaction with my gender, and frustrations about how life works.

Mom may have expected Dad to read her mind about her wants and needs because that's what she tried to do for him. Her motivations most certainly existed outside of her conscious awareness. I know mine did. Acquiring skill in mind reading never occurred to my dad, resulting in many of my mom's wants and needs being left unfulfilled. She didn't know how to advocate for what she wanted, either.

After college I decided to move to another state, returning home periodically to visit. During one of my trips home, I remember dad asking mom to make some Jell-O. We always had a variety of flavors on hand. This time she picked cherry. When my dad sat down for dinner, he asked, "Why didn't you make *orange* Jell-O?" It seemed that nothing Mom did pleased him. In that way, I think he expected her to read his mind, too. She tried hard but she failed just as bad as he did at knowing what she wanted. She couldn't read his mind; he couldn't read hers. Sadly, they never picked up on that fact. They just got mad at each other for failing at it.

Despite these missed attempts at communicating, it never dawned on either of my parents to approach things differently or to get help learning a new way of relating. So, they continued the same old patterns that had been passed down for generations, and my spouse and I followed suit.

When I got married, I believed my husband was a lot different than my dad. And he was. In a lot of ways. He was not a constant yeller like my dad. He wasn't as critical, either. He also liked to travel and do fun things, which I enjoyed doing with him.

I remember deciding, "I am not going to drop what I'm doing just to do what someone else wants me to do like my mom did." Because of that and some other things I changed, I believed I was a lot different than my mom. And I was. In some important ways. I did not become a 'martyr' like my mom (at least not as often as she did), where she consistently gave up what she wanted to please others.

In other words, there were enough variations to camouflage the pattern I was repeating, so I didn't pick up on it. Three decades into my marriage I finally became aware that our relationship replicated many aspects of my parents' ways of interacting. Indeed, I had married someone like my dad, and I had become like my mom...only different.

GRACE FOR ALL OF US

Growing up, it never occurred to me that my parents had once been children and teenagers themselves. I thought they were *always* adults. I had no idea that they had difficulties and struggles during childhood, nor could I comprehend how those experiences shaped them. But after becoming a parent myself, going to therapy, and starting a counseling practice, I had a better understanding of my parents' behavior. As I healed from the pain of my own past, I realized how my dad's traumatic experiences and challenges influenced his behavior. I also understood better why my mom had become passive and shut down.

As a parent, I can understand some of what fueled my dad's quick temper and what caused my mom to withdraw. For a long time, I held onto resentment and unforgiveness for what they *didn't* provide, such as paying for college, buying me a car, or going on vacations. I was jealous of my friends who got those things handed to them from their parents. Until I learned to forgive my parents for what they didn't or couldn't give me, that envy ate at me for several years. It negatively affected me, and the ongoing resentment eventually contributed to the demise of a relationship with some friends who had supportive and generous parents.

It's important to note that by taking an objective look at the factors that shaped our parents and recognizing the baggage that got passed down through the generations to them and to us is not intended to be disrespectful. Nor is it meant to blame them, even though they had faults and made mistakes. For the most part, *they did the best they could with the knowledge and resources available to them.*

Instead, the purpose in reviewing our past is to become aware so *we can change the pattern*. It behooves all of us to forgive our parents. For our own sake, and for the sake of our children! That's the best way to break dysfunctional patterns.

If you are a parent, this is not intended to be a guilt trip. It's a call to become aware. With consciousness, we become empowered to change and improve. When we live in denial of the truth, we perpetuate the problem. Most parents put forth their best efforts, given the struggles they had growing up and the challenges they faced as parents. If I had lived in your family and had your experiences, I probably would have reacted the way you did. In all cases, the love and acceptance we got falls far short of the love we needed. Did you get all the love you needed at the right time and in the right way from your parents? Only God can give that.

As a parent, I did my best. Now that I'm aware of the factors that drove my ditchy behaviors, I realize I made mistakes when raising my children. Overall, my sons are awesome and well-balanced! I also recognize that I'm not solely to blame for their shortcomings. In the past when in my ditch, I took all the responsibility for the problems my children had; then I'd switch and blame my husband for *all* of it. However, now I see that the problems my children faced developed because of many factors, and the same thing is true for all of us. The dysfunction each parent passes on from past generations, siblings, extended family, in-laws, teachers, friends, our own unique ways of reacting, and the media all contribute in some way. In addition, world events, religion, death, accidents, health problems, and lots of other circumstances play a part in affecting how any child grows up.

It's too overwhelming and packed with shame to take all the blame, a proclivity of an OF person. A MF person might not own any of it. "It's all my fault" (OF), and "I didn't do anything!" (MF) are both lies. We find balance when we accurately identify our part and take responsibility for that. It's easier to do that when I see the whole picture and the entire cast of characters involved. Sometimes I carry the lion's share of ownership for the problem; at other times it may be minimal. Practice admitting my mistakes when they're not so big has helped me accept ownership when my errors carry greater magnitude. The truth is, we *all* make both big and little mistakes.

People who experienced harsh consequences or were shamed for misdeeds as children learn to avoid taking ownership when they are wrong because of how they were treated. They may need some healing work to be set free. Many children learned it was too risky to own up to a mistake because they would be severely punished for it. The lesson: It's not safe to tell the truth. It becomes easier to deny wrongdoing, which leads to a deep-seated habit of dishonesty with self and others. As adults, it then requires a lot of work to develop a habit of admitting true feelings and being truthful in general. The habit of lying is hard to break, but with God all things are possible.

As parents, we are faced with many situations we don't know how to handle or don't know what else to do, so our automatic default kicks in. We react without thinking and resort to handling it the way our parents did, saying the kinds of things they said, and punishing in a similar manner to how we were corrected.

If our parents reacted in deep ravine ways (see Chapter 6), we might even blank out when reacting and lose the ability to control our actions. People label that as "dissociation," "compulsive behavior," "abuse," "becoming a victim," or "an addict." Whatever the label, it carries with it a feeling of judgment and shame. I want people to be set free of the labels, so that they feel safe to look at their behavior, take ownership of their part, and with that awareness, move toward empowerment to change. We may not even know where those actions come from because they emanate from our subconscious. Or we may have some awareness of what we are doing in the moment but disconnect from the consequences those actions carry for those around us and ourselves. We may have learned methods of calming down or better ways to discipline such as teaching instead of punishing, but in the heat of the moment all that goes out the window. Once again, we subconsciously switch to default mode.

After the angry outburst, the verbal attack, the aggressive or self-harming behaviors have ended, we return to full consciousness, leaving in the aftermath damage to egos, spirit, or body. It's important in that moment to avoid self-judgment or self-chastisement and instead take an objective look at what happened, what caused the trigger, and then establish a plan to do it a different way next time. Self-criticism only perpetuates the problem and adds to the shame that's already there.

Regarding some issues, I predetermined that I would never be like my parents. In certain circumstances, I decided not to react the way they did, though I didn't think through how I would respond instead. Looking back after my children left home, I realized that in those areas I ended up going to the opposite extreme. Where I concluded that my parents were too harsh, I became too permissive. I didn't want to do what they did but also didn't know a healthier way to address the issue, which landed me in the opposite ditch. This resulted in me saying nothing, condoning behavior I didn't like, or ignoring it altogether. I felt powerless in those moments because I had no pathway to choose a more balanced approach.

In the movie *Catch Me if You Can*, the main character determined to never be poor because his parents divorced over money issues. He succeeded in that. However, because he went to an extreme to accomplish the goal, he, too, ended up alone.

Thinking back, I would have loved for my parents to have had the courage to take a hard look at how their parents treated them, evaluate the factors influencing their situations, and examine how they reacted as a result. Their awareness would have changed how they raised us, and my story would be much different. Had I learned these principles and applied them before I had kids, I would have been a better mom.

However, my lack of awareness and wounding spilled out onto my children. That story is the same for everyone on the planet. God tells us the sins of the fathers are "passed down to the children, to the third and fourth generation of those who hate God" (Exodus 20:5, KJV). Even when we have God in our lives, we often don't act like it. But God "shows mercy to thousands who love God and keep his commandments," so we have an out. We don't have to follow the herd off the cliff or our ancestors into the ditch. We can be the ones who decide to improve our family's legacy. No matter how old we are, it's never too late to change.

Every feeble attempt to shift, God blesses; and the trajectory of our lives draws us closer to the mark.

THE GOOD AND BAD NEWS ABOUT THE WHOLE "OPPOSITES ATTRACT" THING

Every couple I know consists of a member from each ditch.

The fact is, MFs are attracted to OFs, and vice versa. As screwed up as that sounds, it works well when they are "on the road" and able to care for each other's needs and value the thoughts, feelings, concerns, and desires of others and self simultaneously.

Of course, both OFs and MFs possess many strengths born from their natural tendency to be either others- or me-focused. Those are healthy characteristics, which I call "on the road" or "road behaviors." We'll talk about those later. These strengths can complement one another well and produce a harmonious relationship. The following nursery rhyme highlights this idea: "Jack Sprat could eat no fat; his wife could eat no lean. So, together, they licked the platter clean."

Sounds like great teamwork to me!

Even though the focus of this book is about raising awareness and identifying and replacing ditchy actions with healthy ones, recognizing each other's and our own strengths helps us to get out and stay out of the ditch. We will discuss climbing out of the ditch and what being on the road looks like later in this book, so keep reading.

Two MFs wouldn't be able to get along long-term. They'd constantly be fighting to get their own way. Nor would it be likely for two OFs to have a successful relationship. They'd get lost in "I don't know, what do you want?" land. Both would be too hesitant to take the lead. However, I'm speaking in broad generalities. There may be relationships in which both people come from the same ditch; I just haven't run across any yet.

So now we have a match made in heaven.

Or hell.

This is because, while opposites attract and bring different strengths to a relationship, they can also go overboard trying to balance out each other's extremes. Extremes in behavior reveal attempts to find balance. In fact, our opposite strengths can become polarizing.

At times I thought my husband was too strict with the kids, so I became too lenient. Sometimes it went the other way. In some couples, one person might be a neat freak, while the other is a slob. Or one partner is careful with money while the other spends too much. One person drinks too much, and the other becomes a teetotaler. Neither one appreciates what the other does, nor the oblique attempts made by their mate to bring greater balance to the relationship. We both resent the other's extreme and fail to see our own. Neither fully realizes the motivation for their actions; or if they do, they are fearful of stating their desires outright.

And when ditchy reactions outweigh on-the-road behaviors, no matter which ditch we're talking about, the relationship will eventually fall apart.

POINTS TO PONDER

- Fear drives all ditch behaviors.
- The ditchiness comes from our negative pre-programming, which is automatic, subconscious, and reactive.
- When we act without thinking, ditchy behaviors spill out.
- As children, we experienced rejection or abandonment because of what got handed down from past generations, family dynamics, and our unique circumstances.

- Examining how we landed in our ditches, without blaming those who contributed to our predicament, helps us begin the change process.
- Awareness of ditchy behaviors begins the process of figuring out how we might respond in a different way in the future.

Perhaps you identify with OFs or see yourself leaning more towards MF reactions. Maybe you can't decide which ditch to call your "ditch of choice" because you see in yourself tendencies from both.

Hang on. Before your feathers get too ruffled, let's take a look at the great equalizer.

CHAPTER 4

SWITCHING DITCHES

"I Go to Extremes."
—Billy Joel

uring most of my marriage, I identified as the people pleaser, and I could see that my husband lived in the me-focused ditch. Feeling controlled and powerless, I thought he had all the power. I couldn't identify at all with any of his behaviors.

I figured that was the way it was, and that was the way it would always be.

Then one night at a social event, I confessed to a friend, "I feel like I'm walking on eggshells around my husband," not realizing he was standing within earshot.

He jumped in with, "Well, I feel like I walk on eggshells around you, too!"

Shocked, I thought, *What do you mean, you walk on eggshells around me? I'm the one in this family walking on eggshells!*

That night, I discovered a profound truth: When we are off the road and living in ditches, we think we reside only in one ditch, and our partner in the other—but the truth is that we can switch ditches!

What's crazy is that, while this had been happening off and on in my marriage, I had no clue.

How and why do partners change ditches?

Let me explain how it happened to us.

Eventually, the exhaustion of letting others have their way, giving up what I wanted, striving to please, trying to get people to affirm me, trying to do everything for everyone, and resenting feeling obligated to say "yes" all the time pushed me over the edge. I felt driven to try new tactics.

Exasperated, I thought angrily, *Forget you! I'm outta here!*

Furious, I hopped into my little ditch car, turned on that ditch engine, revved it up, and determinedly floored that sucker to scale the steep banks of my people-pleasing ditch. I was heading for the road! By the time my little car's wheels gripped the pavement, the gauge pegged in the red. The acrid smell of exhaust and burnt rubber lingered in the air. Because of the depth of the ditch, it required Dale Earnhardt speed to get out. Except Dale wasn't behind the wheel—I was, and I'm no professional! In my desperate attempt to get away from the frustration, powerlessness, and fear that permeated life in my ditch, the little car spun out of control. I failed to stay on the road, and I couldn't see what lay ahead.

Before I knew what had happened, my little car stopped abruptly, covered with dust, and I found myself in the ditch on the other side of the road. Mind you, I didn't know I'd overcompensated and landed in the MF ditch across the pavement. I thought I was firmly centered in the middle of the road, but the truth is that I didn't have a clue what being on the road even looked like.

Dazed and confused about where I was, and still oblivious to what I was doing, I took on the characteristics of this new ditch. As I looked around, a whole array of reactions beckoned in this place that were absent on the other side. While there, I ignored what others in my life wanted or needed. Unaware that I had missed the road and instead gone into the opposite ditch, *I* became the me-focused one—selfish, controlling, demanding—the same things my spouse did that I hated. I took advantage of all the MF behaviors, oblivious that I had switched extremes, unaware that my actions strangely mirrored those I disliked so much from my spouse, and completely blinded to my me-focused state.

When I landed in that ditch, it was like landing hard on the up side of a teeter totter—with my spouse standing on the lower end. The force of my landing catapulted him out of that ditch as fast as I had entered! And neither of us had a clue about what had happened.

THE GREAT EQUALIZER

I didn't know what I had done, where my spouse went, what caused all the changes, or even that we had switched sides! Our relationship dynamics had always felt confusing to me, and never more so than when I got fed-up with being others-focused and began embracing me-focused behaviors.

I quickly abandoned any thought regarding what my husband wanted or needed. I stopped caring about his perspective at all because I was so focused on my own.

Meanwhile, my husband had fallen under the spell of the OF ditch and began taking on the role of the victim in our relationship. Phrases such as "Fine, do what you want—you're going to, anyway!" "It doesn't matter what I want" and "You don't care about me!" rolled off his lips like he had been an OF all of his life.

Since the opposite ditch isn't as comfortable or familiar to us, we'd hang out there for a little while, then head back "home." This could happen multiple times in a day or go on for stretches of time. During an argument, switching ditches could rival the speed of a ping pong ball during a fast volley. We'd pull out all our ditchy ammunition from both sides and fling it at each other. And—trust me—when you start engaging in ditchy comments and actions, it's a sure way to escalate an argument.

We were married forty years before we ever caught on to our ditch switching. Like sleepwalkers, we passed each other going back and forth. Somehow, this strange routine kept the extremes in our relationship offset, but not happy.

The length of time I spent in the MF ditch depended on how sick I was of my own DOC and how well the MF tactics seemed to be working. Time and time again, desperation drove me to the MF ditch, and discomfort pulled me back.

And I had no idea this was happening. It was a mystery. Until my conversation with my friend about the eggshells cracked the case.

Why had I not picked up on this before?

Discovering the ditch switching blew me away. *How could this be?* After pondering my revelation, I recalled times when I had insisted on my own way without regard to what my husband wanted, had been underhanded and manipulative, became selfish, or grew angry and verbally attacked him. In the trenches of the me-focused ditch, I could be aggressive, controlling, and manipulative.

I'd go to happy hour with my work friends without any thought to what he might want. That was selfish. Our bills had to be handled my way. That was controlling. I yelled when I got frustrated. That was attacking. After becoming aware, an example for almost every ditchy MF behavior popped into my head!

Wow!

Guilty!

Addictions creeped into my life masking as work, relationships, or solitaire—appropriate behaviors turned problematic. These were ways of escaping from my feelings of powerlessness.

I was in the me-focused ditch when I talked my spouse into quitting work and traveling around the United States for two and a half years.

His MF behavior came out when his desire to have a fancy stereo system trumped my wish for a camper.

We ended up with a topper over the truck bed serving as our living quarters. Sleeping bags on insulated mats served as a bedroom, boxes underneath provided storage, and a super high-end stereo offered entertainment for the few months it worked. Essentially, we were backpacking on wheels. With our dog.

Had we been aware of our tendencies to go from one end of the pendulum to the other *and* known how to satisfy both of our wants, we may have ended up with a good stereo *and* a nice place to live while on the road, without the tension. But we didn't know what we were doing, or how to do it any differently. Knowledge of how to find that equilibrium escaped us, and we both ended up defaulting to our preprogrammed reactions.

That's not to say that we didn't have fun. We connected with amazing friends and relatives, toured awesome places, and had great experiences when we were able to agree, which was most of the time. Remember, we just land in the ditches when we don't know how to balance our desires.

The catalysts that propel me to become me-focused are different than what makes my husband me-focused. Looking back, I can see that my husband was more MF about activities, time, work, and logistics. I was more MF about projects.

One person might get me-focused with exercise, work, and TV. The other may be more MF with friends, the house, and the kids. Sometimes it takes a little digging to figure out your MF topics.

My husband and I also differ in *how* we do what we do when in the opposite ditch. I would never think to do to my husband what he does to me. It's also true in reverse. He would never think to do to me what I do to him. Both of us tend to downplay our own actions while magnifying the severity of the other's behavior. At times, my husband employed guilt to get me to do something he wanted; I whined and complained until he gave in. Both tactics were manipulative. I thought what he did was worse than what I did, and I'm sure he felt the opposite way.

In other words, even though we both engaged in the same kinds of ditchy doings, neither of us could see the effects of our actions.

Earlier in our relationship, I didn't have the courage to tell him how I really felt about certain things. He also had difficulty expressing some things to me, but he seemed to have no problem letting me know exactly how he saw "the facts." On certain topics, the adamant part of me also showed up. I didn't see how I discounted him, nor did he catch on to how he devalued my view at times. His angry outbursts may have been more frequent, but I still got angry and blasted him from time to time, too.

We both engage in behaviors from both ditches, but we put our own spin on it. I'd be others focused regarding what my husband wanted to do, what restaurant to pick, or what activities and events to attend. When it came to school, volunteering, cooking, and shopping, I was MF. My withdrawing behaviors tended towards busyness; he became absorbed in TV. He'd get on my case about spending money; I'd bug him about getting things done around the house. One partner might be controlling over finances; the other might complain about how late their spouse works or how much time they spend with friends.

My passive-aggressive behaviors looked different than his. My spouse had expectations around time. I expected him to know what I wanted and how I felt (without me telling him). After all, I reasoned, *If he really loved me or cared, he'd know.*

The *people with whom we switch ditches* also plays a role. It was much easier for me to be angry and lash out at people other than my husband, such as at the kids or customer service representatives. He seemed to have no difficulty expressing his displeasure directly to me.

People can also switch ditches *depending on the relationship.* In a first marriage, an individual may identify as an OF person. When that marriage disintegrates, often the person decides, "I'm never doing that again," and then becomes MF in their second marriage.

An illustration from the movie, *Three Billboards Outside Ebbing, Missouri* shows how we can switch ditches from one relationship to another. Mildred's daughter, Angela, was brutally raped and murdered. Seven months later, Mildred rents three billboards to ask why the police aren't doing anything about it, naming the chief of police (passive aggressive) to spur the police towards taking a more active role in searching for her daughter's killer. As the story unfolds, we discover her ex-husband had been a "wife-beater." He comes to see her for a brief visit, gets triggered, and pushes her against the wall with his hand on her throat, choking her. She obviously is the passive party. The people pleaser. The victim.

As the townspeople polarize and the story continues, Mildred becomes more and more self-focused, unable to see how her actions affect her son, others, or herself. She sets fire to the police station, causing serious burns to a police officer. Who is the attacker now?

Though, she never acted violently towards her husband, she certainly did toward others, but in more indirect ways. She never treated her husband the way he treated her, but her treatment of others got pretty ditchy. Her anger became directed elsewhere when she felt powerless to stand up to her ex-husband's rage. She didn't have a clue what drove her behaviors any more than her ex knew what propelled him to be aggressive towards her.

The *frequency* of these behaviors also shows up in different percentages. Even though I displayed the same MF behaviors (selfish, manipulative, controlling, and angry, for instance), it seemed like my spouse tended towards them more often than I did. If something happened to upset him, he'd be more likely to let it out in the moment, whereas I'd bottle it up until I couldn't hold it in anymore, then blast him for all the resentments accumulated since the last blow-up. He'd pout and feel sorry for himself from time to time, but not stay there long. I'd tend to hang out in martyr mode longer, feeling sorry for myself for sacrificing my wants and desires.

When I felt like I was the victim, I was convinced that my spouse was the one to blame, the one at fault, the one who had the issues. I didn't see my part at all. Little did I know that he felt victimized by me too, but in different ways, on different topics, and with different reactions!

When we'd get into arguments, we'd pull ammunition from both ditches. Every escalated disagreement that ended unresolved for the umpteenth time could be traced to fear and feeling powerless. That's the fuel that propels the bus. Once that is understood, the number of conflicts and their intensity can be reduced significantly, just by knowing what to do differently. You'll learn how to address fears in Chapter 16.

We need to advocate for cleaner-burning fuel! Fear and powerlessness pollute the emotional environment. Let's all become environmentalists when it comes to relationships. To be driving down the road empowered by God's Spirit is much more economical than being stuck in a ditch somewhere fueled by fear. And it's a lot more fun!

Once I became aware of switching ditches, I started taking ownership for the ditchy behaviors I engaged in from both sides. Though it manifested in different ways, varied depending on circumstances, looked dissimilar, fluctuated in intensity, and changed from person to person, I have been stuck in both ditches!

That truth was a tough pill to swallow!

Here's what switching ditches looks like:

OTHERS-FOCUSED   ME-FOCUSED

Switching Ditches

| | Thoughts
Feelings
Concerns
Desires | Conscious
Mindful
Aware
Balanced | Thoughts
Feelings
Concerns
Desires | |

Subconscious
Automatic
Pre-Programmed
Reaction

OTHERS-FOCUSED

1. People Pleaser
2. Default answer: yes
3. Readily give up what I want
4. Difficulty making decisions
5. Eggshells
6. Difficulty expressing thoughts/feelings
7. Avoiding
8. Co-dependent
9. Blaming
10. Passive
11. Obligated
12. Resentful
13. Sarcastic
14. Criticize/gossip
15. Hurt
16. Passive-Aggressive
17. Withdraw
18. Shut down
19. Chaotic
20. Victim
21. Self-harming

ME-FOCUSED

1. Selfish
2. Default answer: no
3. Perfectionism
4. I'm right
5. Difficulty seeing other perspective
6. Demanding
7. Manipulative
8. Critical
9. Controlling
10. Vocal about feelings
11. Expectations
12. Disappointment
13. Angry
14. Demeaning
15. Threatening
16. Yelling
17. Attacking/accusing
18. Rigid
19. Addicted
20. Physical attacks
21. Harming others

Extreme
Powerless
Fear

Greatest fear: rejection
Tendency: to abandon
Difficult to admit: I allowed that

Extreme
Powerless
Fear

Greatest fear: abandonment
Tendency: to reject
Difficult to admit: I did that

Remember, every ditch behavior is an extreme, because we don't know how to find the middle ground and address the issue in a balanced way. It stems from fear that we won't get what we want. We are both seeking love and acceptance while simultaneously trying to protect ourselves from being rejected or abandoned.

I subconsciously believed I was unlovable and was convinced that if anyone knew the real me, I would be kicked to the curb and rejected. Because I believed that, I acted as though it was true. In trying to protect myself from rejection by abandoning before I could be rejected, I unwittingly pulled it into my life by my actions!

The same is true for an MF's fear of being left. Because they believe they will be abandoned, they act in rejecting ways to protect themselves. They don't feel loved or accepted for who they are any more than OFs do. Others then end up abandoning them because of their abrasive, attacking ways.

Once we become aware of what we've been doing, the most difficult truth for an adult OF to accept is "I allowed that." The greatest challenge for a MF to reconcile is "I did that."

And we switch ditches! We alternate between fear of abandonment and fear of rejection. Therefore, sometimes we act in rejecting ways and at other times we act in abandoning ways. Therefore, we must grapple with the fact that we at times allowed behaviors we shouldn't have and other times we did things that hurt others. It's a wonder any relationship ever survives!

POINTS TO POINDER

- When our tactics in one ditch fail to be successful, we switch ditches and go to the other extreme.
- Though the *type* of behavior is the same, what we do looks different than what our partner does.

- The way the ditch behavior manifests, with whom, the frequency, and the topic all influence our ditch-switching tendencies.
- We all have a DOC, our default mode of reacting.
- Depending on the topic, this transfer can happen multiple times in one conversation.
- We attempt to protect from rejection by withdrawing (abandoning).
- We attempt to avoid abandonment by rejecting.
- Difficult truths to accept: "I allowed that" and "I did that."
- Because we switch ditches, we are guilty of doing both OF and MF ditchy things.

How could I stop this ditch-switching madness?

Before looking for a way out, let's learn about what's behind the stress, hurt, and anger of people stuck in ditches.

CHAPTER 5

EVERYONE IS AFRAID

"Everyone is afraid of something."
—Cassandra Clare

*I*n Chapter 3, we looked at the fears driving ditch behaviors. This chapter is devoted to examining at deeper level four prevalent ways that fear manifests. The most common places it hides is beneath anger, rage, hurt, and stress.

I've already mentioned that fear likes to run under the radar, like a stealth jet. While it remains undetected, it can work freely and wreak havoc.

None of us are exempt from the deception of fear. Even I am often too blinded by my own concerns to see it, despite the fact I'm in the business of helping others identify their worries.

On a recent flight, a woman seated next to me commented, "I don't like to fly."

That started a conversation where I mentioned a tapping process called emotional freedom technique (EFT), which could help reduce her fear of flying.

She quickly retorted, "Oh, I'm not afraid."

Really? I thought to myself. *Then why don't you like to fly?*

People averse to flying generally feel claustrophobic, concerned about a plane crash, worried about turbulence, or generally anxious. *Those are all variations of fear!*

The woman's reaction to my comment mirrors my own tendencies to deny feeling afraid. When that happens, fear can merrily go about its business of keeping me uneasy and anxious.

When clients talk about feeling angry, I ask, "What is your fear?"

They typically respond with some variation of, "I'm not afraid, I'm just mad!"

The critical point here involves conscious awareness of the emotion, leading to a thought-out response, instead of a knee-jerk reaction driven by fear.

Instead of allowing fear to drive his behavior, Jesus took note of how He felt, and thought through the most effective way to address the money changers in the temple (see John 2:14–15 ESV). Most of the time when we experience anger, we allow fear to motivate us instead of evaluating the best course of action. While it is true that we are justified in feeling upset about something that has happened, our distress (a synonym of fear) often drives the feeling, leading to behaviors we regret later. The individual remains in a powerless state, and fear drives the bus, causing us to react in unhealthy ways, which ultimately do not produce the desired results.

If you don't believe that fear hides beneath anger, consider the example of a child playing in the front yard with a parent. The ball rolls out into the street and the child runs after it. The parent sees an oncoming car and screams at the child to stop, feeling terror at the possibility of the child getting hit. Then, the minute the child is safe, the parent's anger takes over and the child gets a royal rant about never going into the street again without stopping to check for cars first.

In the United States, and many parts of the world, men are taught not to be "sissies." From the time they are young boys, they are ridiculed, shamed, and put down when they admit to having fear. This approach has been passed down for generations. The result: they learn to hide how scared they feel inside, and then it grows and leaks out as anger. By the time boys become men, there is a giant disconnect between the reaction of anger and the initial experience of fear. Oddly, it is socially acceptable for men to show anger, as long as they don't show fear!

It's one thing to acknowledge and face the fear, and another to push it down. That's a subtle, but significant, difference. Any time we bungee jump, ride a roller coaster, or try anything new that we've never done before, there's an element of angst that we recognize, but then we decide it's worth the risk and go forward.

Fear exists on a continuum. Sometimes it is mild, and other times we're shaking-in-our-boots scared. When we allow ourselves to acknowledge the feeling, calculate the risks, and then decide to proceed anyway, we overcome the spirit that wants to hold us back. That's a healthy way to deal with fear, and it is exhilarating when we overcome it.

When we fail to acknowledge the fear and suppress it instead, it's held down much like a beach ball under water. It can be submerged only so long before our arms grow tired or a wave comes along and pushes the ball out from under the pressure keeping it beneath the surface. It explodes upward, with water spraying in all directions. That's exactly what fear does when it explodes via an angry outburst or in a rage. The person doesn't know what drove the reaction, only the situation that set it off. It could be triggered by getting cut off in traffic, someone using the same tone that a parent used when the adult was eight years old, a color reminding of some past horror, a sound linking to a past trauma, or a smell triggering recall of a nightmarish memory. That's why traumatized veterans may dive under a table when they hear a loud boom. However, we don't have to go off to war to be affected in the same way.

My mate's anger often leaked out at me, or at least it *felt* like it was directed at me, even though it probably wasn't as often as I thought it was. Every time it happened, it harkened back to when my dad yelled at me when I was a kid, and I re-experienced those same feelings.

Men are taught that it's manly to be "unemotional," but that really means to squelch all feelings except anger. Emotions have become flatlined.

In the military, soldiers are conditioned to be courageous, and rightly so. That goes for our first responders as well: firemen, policemen, SWAT teams, emergency medical technicians, doctors, and nurses. They have all been gifted with the ability to put emotions aside to attend to the task at hand. I'm deeply grateful for the Godly calling they have. Their gift amazes me. Thank you to all of you in these categories! It takes a lot of bravery to do what you do every day.

Just because these professionals don't acknowledge emotions when on duty doesn't mean they don't have them. Like the rest of us, it's critically important for them to have a healthy way to deal with their feelings. Inroads are being made to help these everyday heroes, and counseling is offered after significant traumatic disasters, but it's woefully insufficient to deal with the accumulation of traumas they experience daily.

While talking about it is helpful, it doesn't ultimately clear out the lies, fears, and negative beliefs about the experience held by our inner parts. Any approach that gets at our subconscious, where we store those memories, helps clear out trauma. Examples of modalities that address the subconscious include Emotional Freedom Technique (EFT); Eye Movement Desensitization Reprocessing (EMDR); metaphors; various therapies such as sand tray, art, equine, experiential, psychodrama, gestalt, inner healing prayer, Internal Family Systems (IFS), hypnotism, and Rapid Resolution Therapy (RRT). There are also other approaches with which I'm not familiar that get at our subconscious as well. It is important to find a therapist who will help you process what is stored in your subconscious.

In talking to a first responder, I asked, "What's the worst experience you ever had?"

He responded, "In what category? Decapitations, gruesome injuries, burns, car accidents, shootings, stabbings, domestic violence? At the station we joke about those things with each other to diffuse the impact."

Realizing the magnitude of emotional impact that first responders deal with every day felt overwhelming to me. They become desensitized to it, just like we have by school shootings, unless we are directly affected by one. However, that's a lot of bottled up, unprocessed emotions that eventually leak out *somehow* unless they get resolved.

Let's take a look at several manifestations of unprocessed emotions:

ANGER

What lies behind anger?

Anger is driven by frustration, guilt, insecurity or inferiority, sadness or trauma. Under each of these feelings lies fear, the third level down. No wonder we don't connect it with anger! Most of the time we don't associate feeling angry with anything other than our belief that *someone else* caused us to have an outburst!

Let's take a closer look at a few of the fears that are often driving the feelings of guilt, insecurity, frustration, trauma or sadness. This is not an exhaustive list, but hopefully it's enough to get you thinking about what specific *fears*—and there may be many—drive the anger you've experienced in the past.

Frustration:
- Not getting what you want
- Things not working out the way you want
- Missing a deadline
- Taking on more than you can handle
- Not knowing how to do something

Guilt:
- Getting caught
- Shame
- Exposure
- Punishment or consequences

Insecurity or inferiority:
- Not being good enough
- Others being better
- Being ridiculed, put down, or criticized

- Not being safe
- Being wrong

Sadness or grief:
- Never going away
- Loss
- Things never getting better
- Never being happy again

Trauma:
- Happening again
- Getting hurt
- Pain
- Shame or humiliation
- Remembering

The purpose of identifying and naming the fears helps ferret them out of hiding so you can catch them and send them away. Once you've named them, check out Chapter 16 to find resolution in the most effective manner possible.

RAGE

Now, let's talk about anger on steroids. Extreme feelings of powerlessness incite rage, defined as violent, uncontrollable anger. An element of dissociation fits here, because the individual momentarily loses control of his or her own actions.

Anger and rage spill out on others and manifest as outward aggression.

We deal with rage in the same way as anger, by identifying the fears fueling it, then acting to resolve them, which we will discuss at length in the second half of the book.

HURT

Now let's move over to the passive ditch. Not identifying with anger at all, I tended towards feeling hurt. That was my M.O. If something happened that bothered me, I would keep silent about it and store it up. Because my outbursts occurred infrequently, I tended to forget about how the bottled-up hurt accumulated and fermented for weeks, then exploded all over my husband from time to time. I ran on a low-grade hurt level, much like my father and husband carried chronic low-grade anger. My hurt was directed inward toward myself most of the time.

What fears could possibly be hiding behind hurt? An individual who feels hurt has experienced an injury, which may be physical, mental, emotional, or all three combined. On top of the wound, fears rush in: fear that I deserved what I got, that it's all I'm ever going to get, that I'll never get what I want, that the pain will get worse or never go away, that I will never have enough money, that I'm unloved, unwanted, abandoned, or rejected, especially by God.

There are as many fears masking hurt as there are disguising anger.

STRESS

Though there are probably lots of other places you can find fears hiding, our last big rock in this chapter to look beneath is stress. Everyone experiences stress. It's common to hear people talk about feeling "stressed out." I've spent a lot of my life feeling stressed. It usually goes hand-in-hand with feeling overwhelmed.

Five decades of my life passed before I caught on to the culprits pushing my stress buttons. Until this discovery took place, stress to me felt like a thick, heavy, gray blanket pushing down on me. Some unseen forces seemed to be holding it by its four corners, stretched out over my head just out of reach. Meanwhile, I had no power to move the blanket or make it go away. It was just there, relentlessly pushing down on me.

One evening while working on my undergraduate degree, I had a paper due the next day, both of my kids needed help with homework, and my husband called for help with a project. I felt overwhelmed and worried about all that needed to be done. By some divine intervention, instead of becoming a testy snapping turtle with my family like I normally did when feeling stressed, I stopped and took stock of what was going on. I asked myself why I felt so stressed. It boiled down to fear that I would not have time to get my paper done.

I took a moment, analyzed the many demands on my time, and assessed how much time each task required. I figured that my kids only needed me for about an hour, and my spouse just needed my help with one small thing. I reprioritized my time and decided to help my children with their schoolwork first, then assisted my husband with his project, leaving the remainder of the evening free to concentrate on my assignment. The moment I identified the fear behind the stress and came up with a plan to complete what needed to be done, the stress suddenly dissipated!

Since that pivotal event, every time I feel stressed (which still occurs regularly), I have a strategy to deal with it. Paul Simon may have "50 Ways to Leave Your Lover," but I've got twenty-four ways to ditch your fears!

Hurt and stress tend to show up in the others-focused ditch, while anger and rage can be found in the me-focused ditch. We're all affected by fear. Because we switch ditches, we also go back and forth between directing it toward self or others. When I'm not balanced and on the road, I hang out probably 80 percent of the time in my default ditch, leaving about 20 percent of the time in which my ditchy ways align with the MF ditch. However, at the end of the day, it's all fear. It just manifests in different ways.

When we climb out of the murky, cloudy ditch onto the road, we find freedom from fear. "There is no **fear** in love [dread does not exist], but full-grown (complete, perfect) love turns **fear** out of doors *and* expels every trace of terror! For **fear** brings with it the thought of punishment, and [so] he who is afraid has not reached the full maturity of love [is not yet grown into love's complete perfection]" (1 John 4:18, AMPC, emphasis mine). If I have fear, it means I haven't yet learned how to trust God in that area. It often occurs related to something we did not feel protected by God in the past. Once I recognize that, I can ask God to teach me how to trust him and let go of the fear, despite my past experience.

If we can start recognizing fear for what it is, we may have more compassion for our partners. Instead of alternating our assessment of them between "monster" and "mouse," we may begin seeing them for the wounded little girls and boys they are inside their grown-up bodies. That's difficult to do when we're thickly caked with anger and hurt!

In the next chapter, we will discuss how people who have been oppressed for generations under powerlessness and fear land in deep ravines. But we won't stop there; we're going to help them find a way out!

POINTS TO PONDER:

- All of us experience hidden fears that manifest as anger, rage, hurt, and stress.
- Anger's secondary emotions include guilt, inferiority, insecurity, frustration, trauma, and sadness.
- Powerlessness and fear drive those emotions.

- We either turn against ourselves when we feel hurt or against others when angry.
- Stress can be overcome by identifying fears and addressing them.
- Love is the opposite of fear and God can help us overcome the fear.

CHAPTER 6

DEEP RAVINES

"When a blind man leads a blind man
They both end up in a ditch."
—*Matt. 15:14 (MSG)*

$\mathcal{I}$f you grew up in a home where any of the behaviors listed in Appendix occurred, it was *normal* for you. That doesn't mean it was right, good, or to be replicated. That was how your family reacted to their powerless feelings because they didn't know any other way.

It's important to understand where these ditchy ways of relating started, so the shame of experiencing and replicating some of these behaviors in your own life can be removed. Shame and guilt keep us locked into negative patterns. Awareness, conscious actions, and work on forgiving others and self can set us free to create a new framework of relating in our families.

The ditchy ways your family related didn't begin with you, your parents, or even their parents. It's been going on for generations.

The good news is that these ineffective ways of relating can stop with *you*. However, we can't end something that exists outside of our awareness or that we are actively hiding, which is why it's important to take an objective look (without judging or shaming your parents or yourself) at what happened in your childhood and what filtered down into your life or parenting. It's never too late to make improvements!

When traumatic things happen to us as little children, we cope in the best way we can. Our options typically include:

- talking about it (but how can we do that when we are too young to have words?)
- internalizing blame (we come to believe that it was our fault and we deserved it, which leads to self-harming and suicidal behaviors)
- denial ("I wasn't abused in any way")
- minimizing ("it wasn't that bad")
- blocking it out ("I had a great childhood; nothing bad ever happened!")
- developing a part of self to carry the trauma and another part to handle the anger (dissociation).

Some of these factors lead to behaviors we don't realize we do.

Notice that a lot of the coping methods I just mentioned are variations of not remembering. We may not recall the incidents, the feelings connected to what happened, or important aspects of the events, but our subconscious knows. When something happens that touches on those bad experiences, we become triggered and react automatically. We then do to our children what happened to us. Sometimes, through our words or actions, we are unaware that we are harming our children in similar ways our parents hurt us. We wanted something different but didn't know how to achieve it. We were stuck in a deep ravine with no apparent pathway out!

You may discover striking similarities between what happened to you as a child and what you did in a moment of uncontrollable anger as an adult. That's the importance of raising awareness about what we experienced.

Hope is on the way! We *can* change. Even if your kids are grown and out of the house, they will be blessed by your efforts to improve.

The behaviors we'll talk about in this chapter come from "deep ravines." Allow me to explain why. Born and raised in flat farming country where an overpass is considered a major hill, I freak out on steep, narrow mountain roads.

Therefore, driving down Mount St. Helens, Washington, on the Spirit Lake side took great determination, all my attention, and white knuckles to accomplish.

It would have been easy if the mountain had formed walls on both sides of the road, but it didn't. A steep ravine on one side taunted me all the way down. I could just see myself veering off the road, tumbling end over end in my vehicle until finally it crashed on the bottom, far away from the road where no one could see. Worse yet, where I saw depressions in the road, I imagined those spots forming sinkholes, suddenly giving way just as I drove over and propelling my car and me into the abyss below. I could imagine being violently tossed around, my head banging on the windshield, tasting the blood running down my face, feeling my bones break. That's what I imagined it would be like falling into a ravine.

Once safely at the bottom of the two-lane descent and back on the main road, my right knee shook uncontrollably. I could almost taste the fear; I could certainly feel it.

Some roads give way to deep ravines, like narrower versions of the Grand Canyon. These are death traps for the unaware driver. To stay between the lines, full attention must be devoted to the road. We can't be drunk, stoned, texting, or looking inside the car for some object while driving without the risk of plummeting off the road.

However, there are times we engage in one or more of those types of activities, and the potential consequences don't even cross our minds. Suddenly, we wake up in the hospital. Or we land at the bottom of a ditch or ravine. Dazed, we ask ourselves, *What happened?* It is only upon reflection that we piece together the circumstances that led to the mishap. Sometimes, the accident is so bad that memory of the incident is completely obscured from our consciousness.

Deep ravines symbolize extreme behaviors that are hurtful to both others and to us. Indeed, any time I cause pain for someone else, I also harm myself, and vice versa, whether I'm aware of the injury I cause or not.

Our society has become sensitized to the term "abuse." Every day in the news, we hear some account of violence done to another. Indeed, it *is* abuse. However, when what I have lived through is labeled "abuse," suddenly I feel intense shame, like there is something inherently wrong with me, as though I caused the abuse somehow. A "shame storm," as Brené Brown terms it, washes over me when I recognize some area in which I failed in a big way.[1] For example, when I lash out in anger, afterwards I feel humiliated for what I said.

The first few years in my therapy practice, when a behavior fell into the category of a deep ravine, I'd whip out the list of abusive behaviors and encourage my client to go through and highlight the behaviors they had experienced from others and then note what defensive reactions the client had used. This was intended to help to raise awareness. Too often, I'd never see those people again.

Then I thought back to my own experience. It was easy to admit that I grew up in a house where my dad yelled a lot. Until I was in my thirties, I was unaware that it was verbal abuse. I vividly remember the day I put the two together. Immediately, it felt like a bucket of iced shame suddenly got dumped on my head. I did whatever I could to avoid confessing the truth that I had grown up in an abusive household. It felt like I was inherently bad. After that, I realized that clients must feel the same way when their experience is labeled "abuse," even when it's true. However, as I've been studying ditch behaviors, I've learned that *all* of us experience the ditchy actions of others, and we've also dished it out. If I say an unkind word to someone, I'm guilty of being in the ditch. If I act out of fear or feeling powerless in any way, I'm in the ditch. So that evens the score. We're all ditch people; it's just a matter of degree. The ditchier our family was, the steeper the ravine we're in, and the longer the path to climb out.

But we can all climb out!

When fighting escalates to yelling, name calling, throwing things, destruction of personal property, or physical or sexual abuse, that's evidence that people are stuck in deep ravines. In one ditch you'll find the angry, aggressive, controlling, or domineering individual. In the opposite ditch lies the hurt, compliant, avoidant, and passive victim. Usually the latter has some awareness of their feeling of powerlessness, though it may not be fully conscious.

However, everyone thinks that the controlling, domineering person has all the power. At some level that is true, but underneath the rage and aggressive behavior is also a feeling of powerlessness. The whole reason for engaging with such violence, whether by words or actions, is to cover up that feeling of powerlessness. And remember, we switch ditches; therefore, our ditchy reactions come from both sides. What both have in common is feelings of powerlessness and not knowing how to change the dynamic.

It took a long time for me to figure that out.

Usually, though not always, the partner in the passive ditch is the one who seeks therapy. Perhaps the person most often the target of abuse is the one who feels the most miserable. The other partner maintains an illusion of being in control because the bullying behavior gets that individual what they *think* they want. However, shame for acting that way spins the cycle.

Anger grows out of fear. The stronger the fear, the bigger the feeling of powerlessness to do something about it. That leads to knee-jerk reactions and use of force to attempt to regain control. Yelling comes from not feeling heard, spurred on by inability to effectively get the other person to understand and act on their wishes. Most of us didn't get a model for healthy interactions. What we got was a template for arguing, yelling, manipulating, shaming, or coercing to achieve compliance. Most of us didn't grow up with Foster Kline and Jim Faye guiding us on *Parenting with Love and Logic* or with Cloud and Townsend teaching us *Boundaries*.

In one extreme ravine you'll find people lashing out at those close to them in violent ways. That can show up in a barrage of attacking words: "You are stupid!" "What's the matter with you?" "There, you did it again!" "How many times do I have to tell you to get it through your thick head?" "You don't think!" Though very hurtful, those attacks are mild compared to the words way too many kids hear: "You good for nothing piece of crap!" "I'm sorry I had you!" "I hate you!" "Go away!"

Labels push us further down the ravine: "Slut." "Lazy ass." "Stupid." "Good for nothing." "Idiot." You get the idea. People who have suffered all kinds of abuse state that words can hurt way more than a physical beating because they stay with us, and when we become adults, we replay those messages in our heads over and over.

Violence can also show up in actions: pushing, hair pulling, kicking, blocking exits, pinning down, hitting, punching, pinching, scratching, beating, whipping, breaking, raping, molesting, road raging, throwing things, and destroying property, especially things you know the other person cherishes. The list in Appendix is much more extensive. It's helpful to recognize the reactions to which family members resorted during their fits of rage and feeling extreme powerlessness. These behaviors tumble us to the bottom of the ravine and make it very difficult to get up.

People can also do violence against themselves. This most often happens when children lived in deep ravines growing up because they were powerless to stand up to the attacks levied on them. They were victims. It is what they learned. Internally, they believed they were "bad," they "deserved it," or they "caused it." None of those messages were true, but that's what they were told or concluded. Once these children grow up, their internal critic continues to remind them of these beliefs and, as a result, many turn to self-harming behaviors. They manifest as: anorexia, bulimia, cutting, attempts at suicide or self-injury, reckless driving, smoking, drinking, overeating, doing drugs, and sexual promiscuity, just to name some of the most common ways people punish themselves.

Likewise, it seems that the more we have been traumatized, the less aware of the present we tend to be. We get lost in the past or caught up in a fantasy future, often switching between the two. Or, we oscillate from agonizing about painful memories to fretting or daydreaming about what might happen in the days, months, or years ahead. More frequently than we recognize, something traumatic has happened to us, and our subconscious may or may not block it from conscious memory. Sometimes, our brains become absorbed with negative feelings, fears, or events of the past.

Whether we have memory of it or not, we go through life without realizing how the conclusions we drew about what we experienced impact the decisions we make *today*. We believe "it's in the past," "it doesn't bother me now," or "I don't remember it," and therefore conclude that we've moved on and it doesn't affect us that much. All of these may be true if we just check in with our brain, but our subconscious may tell us a different story.

Those were the kinds of things I said after I had "gotten past" the sudden loss of my grandmother when I was fourteen and my nine-year-old brother a month after graduating high school at age eighteen.

After the funerals were over, "I got over it" and "moved on with my life." In college, I attributed my inability to concentrate and the need to reread every page several times to "uninteresting subjects." Over thirty years later, after extensive therapy, attending recovery groups, reading self-help books, and becoming a counselor, I realized that my lack of comprehension had more to do with the trauma I had suffered than it had to do with class content. Those losses had an even greater impact on what I concluded about relationships. Through death, my grandmother and brother abandoned me, which created an intense fear of abandonment, on top of already feeling rejected because of the early childhood experiences we already discussed. The more I cared about someone, the greater the double-bind I felt, and the more intense the fear became. My childhood experience proved I would either be rejected or abandoned. I tried to hedge against both and failed miserably.

Little did I know that over time those losses contributed to blocking my feelings, depression, and adopting unhealthy coping mechanisms. I fled the scene of my emotional wreckage but didn't realize I dragged the pieces with me everywhere I went. Scientists have discovered that our frontal lobe, the thinking, reasoning part of our brain, is affected when we experience significant trauma.[2]

Now that the trauma has healed, I don't have any problem with reading or comprehension and have overcome my fears of rejection and abandonment, though it still hurts when someone either rejects or abandons me. I've certainly been guilty of doing that to many people about whom I deeply cared, whether intentionally or unintentionally (most of the time it was the latter).

With the effects I experienced related to my losses, I wonder how many kids get diagnosed with disorders because they have difficulty comprehending and attending, but are actually suffering trauma from the results of a disrupted life, such as going through a divorce; experiencing physical, verbal, or sexual abuse; or being bullied at school?

Let's examine what reactions from traumatic experiences might look like in everyday relationships and what categorizes them as deep ravines. These are examples of situations and common (over-)reactions triggered by past traumas: "If he goes out without me, I freak out." "If I've had a stressful day, I reach for a drink, or three, to calm my nerves." "If she spends too much, I yell." "If I'm upset, I can't eat." "If we have an argument, I storm out of the house." "If I'm overwhelmed, I can't think." "When I feel depressed, I eat a carton of ice cream." "If someone cuts me off in traffic, I tailgate super close." "If I'm in a rage, I throw things, punch a hole in the wall, or start swinging." "If I'm depressed, I stay in bed all day." "If I'm nervous, I pop an antacid, Prozac, or Valium."

Each of the above have one thing in common: only quasi-conscious thought went into the behavior. These ways of coping reveal that individual's best attempt to deal with a situation. It seems to them that no other options exist. Remember that ditch behaviors include any response that is an extreme, where we either only think of others, or only consider ourselves. We're not able to navigate both simultaneously when in the ditch. Only when on the road can we see both ditches well enough to consider both the other person's *and* our own perspective at the same time.

Not knowing how to balance one's own needs with the needs of others, we tend to either default to what others want without regard to how it affects us, or focus on ourselves and our desires, oblivious to how it impacts others. People coming from deep ravines typically had only three options available to them as children when something distressing happened: fight, take flight, or freeze.[3] We have all employed these responses at different times and in varying degrees in our own lives. We may or may not be aware when we do. The less aware we are, the more reactive we are. Our comebacks are automatic, employed without thinking, and come from embedded programming. We don't just grow out of our traumatic reactions; they stay with us until we deal with and heal from the experiences that caused them.

Let's take a closer look at these three automatic reactions.

FIGHT

When aggressive behavior is rewarded, a habit of fighting to get our way when feeling threatened may develop. The prize:

others backed down, gave us what we wanted, or at least avoided us so we would be left alone. It may have stemmed from the model we got from our caregivers. A child may have witnessed violence in the home and saw two options: be the aggressor or be the victim. The one wielding the most force seemed to have the upper hand; therefore, the child adopts this stance.

However, using this kind of defense comes from a deep, subconscious feeling of powerlessness and lack of control over one's own emotions. It is very deceptive. Up until recently, I thought people who were controlling, angry, or violent were powerful. Indeed, their "power" is based on intimidation. They become bullies as children and narcissists or terrorists as adults. Inside, they are full of fear, insecurity, and self-hatred, feel emotionally out of control, and have very fragile egos.

Behaviors that land us in this type of ravine involve any kind of physical force. Please refer to the Appendix for examples.

Threats or injury to other people, animals, or destroying property come from deep ravine knee-jerk reactions. These types of behaviors reveal how desperately afraid the abuser is and how small they must feel on the inside to resort to such demeaning tactics. People who regularly engage in these behaviors are truly unaware of how miserable they make themselves feel while trying to be in control.

People may cower in fear and give them what they want, but it does not lead to peace, contentment, or close relationships. In fact, it ensures that the person who does these kinds of things *will* be miserable, anxious, isolated, and alone. The recipients feel traumatized, walk on eggshells, and resort to flight or freeze reactions. This is their best attempt to cope, because fighting back only brings on more dire consequences.

FLIGHT

Fleeing an uncomfortable, destructive, or emotionally painful situation is another frequent reaction. Our nature may not be aggressive, we may be weaker than our opponent, we may have no way of discussing a topic without causing conflict, or we may be afraid of getting hurt either physically or emotionally. Therefore, the best option is to escape.

The people more likely to feel hurt than angry are the ones who tend to flee. They don't like confrontation and avoid it as much as possible. They go to their room, storm off, get on their motorcycle and peel out, drive for hours in their car, go shopping, exercise, get involved with something outside the home, or head for the refrigerator, bottle, pills, or the arms of another person. . .*anything* to calm their anxiety, which they may not even recognize exists.

FREEZE

People who react by freezing couldn't escape as a child. Attempts to resist their attacker failed. Where could they go? Nowhere. The best defense became compliance, to get through it faster or to suffer the least. Putting up a fight resulted in more pain than it was worth. All the escape routes were closed to the hapless victim.

Freezing can look like someone who just sits there, appearing "checked out." Indeed, they are. Their mind went somewhere else while the trauma was happening. As adults, anything that triggers a disturbing memory causes a dissociative reaction.

Ability to dissociate becomes perfected over time. The person may not even know when it's happening. Family and friends around them most of the time don't pick up on it either.

Others may notice the person is acting different but are unable to comprehend why.

Common statements that could tip us off are often overlooked: "Didn't you hear me when I told you I was going to be gone on Tuesday?" "You look like you're daydreaming." "Don't just sit there, say something!" "You seem lost in thought."

Each of these could be indicators of some type of dissociation. Or not. We could just have something else on our mind. It could be as benign as thinking about what to make for dinner. Therefore, I can't assume dissociation is the culprit when my spouse doesn't remember to pick up milk on the way home after I've asked. He could have just been distracted.

The only way we can know what *is* going on is by *asking*. The same is true when I get lost in thought. Preoccupation means we aren't fully aware in the current moment; our mind is somewhere else. Where is it? If I don't know where it is, I need to find it and figure out what makes it go MIA and why. What triggered it to leave?

When my kids were young, before getting the healing I needed from my past experiences, I often got lost in my thoughts. Driving to piano practice one day, my son asked, "Mom do you have a lot on your mind?"

Snapped out of my preoccupation, I thoughtfully responded, "Well, yes, I guess I do! Why?"

He said, "You should go on the Mind Eraser!"

He had recently been to the amusement park and gone on several roller coasters, one of them named Mind Eraser. I wish it were that simple. Triggers alert brains to disappear from present awareness because of something that reminds us of a disturbing memory. It can be anything that links us back to the trauma: a color, smell, time of year, tone, phrase, movement, object, place, or feeling.

Boom! We are teleported to the trauma that shook our world faster than Scotty could beam up Spock in *Star Trek*. The event may even be blocked from our memory, but something residual remains, and suddenly our reactions stem from the memory instead of the current situation.

How do we climb out of a deep ravine? The same way we climb out of any ditch. Start by noticing. Take note of what you do and how you react. Tune in to what thoughts run through your mind. Ask a close family member to help you notice. Jot down the times you've been triggered to fight, flee, or freeze. What happened just before that? What stimulated your reaction? You probably landed in the ravine because this kind of thing has been going on in your family for generations. This is your opportunity to break the cycle. It requires letting go of the shame that has kept you there.

How *do* we let go of shame? It is a process. We begin by making a conscious decision that holding onto shame no longer serves me. Giving it to God helps a lot. Of course, we'll take it back fifty times before we truly begin to trust that we can let it go! Going to Christ-centered recovery groups help us realize that we are not alone. Seeking therapy that gets at the subconscious can be transformational. It also helps to work on forgiving others for what happened to you and forgive yourself for your part, no matter how small that might be. Sometimes our part is "I was there," or "I was too terrified to say anything." Talk therapy can help, but it can't clear out the stuff we store underground.

As we've already discussed, awareness is the first step. When raised in homes where ditch behaviors exist (i.e., all homes, though some are worse than others; it's just on a continuum), those actions are normal to us, and we don't even know those behaviors are ditchy. An extensive (though not exhaustive) list of ditch behaviors can be found in the Appendix. It exists to help you understand the ditch behaviors you experienced growing up so that you can begin the process of eradicating them from your own life.

For example, as kids, when my sister and I fought, there would be scratching, hair pulling, punching, calling names. All something that happened. All normal. All ditchy. Now that I know that, I don't do those things anymore. That is my desire for you too. I want to help you let go of those actions that keep you stuck in a ravine. Chances are, you didn't even know they were ditch behaviors!

You may be surprised to see the pattern. What was done to you frequently gets repeated without you even realizing it. But we can't stop it unless we recognize it. So, let go of the shame and do yourself a favor. Admit to yourself the truth and let yourself out of the darkness of hiding. Then pick *one* thing to work on changing.

An experience illustrating the slow change process is when my husband and I quit our jobs and traveled around the US. I believed in prayer, but it did not occur to me to pray or ask for God's involvement in accomplishing that dream.

Fully *a year and a half* after we made the decision to sell our house and travel, it finally popped in my mind to start praying about it. Then, after God answered that prayer and blessed us with that incredible opportunity, I forgot to pray for other needs as they arose. Six months into our trip, we ran out of our allocated savings. I hit the panic button. "Oh, no! We're going to have to quit traveling and be like real people and get a job!"

Then, a while later I thought to pray about it. God provided, again. As our travels continued, the length of time between hitting the panic button and thinking to pray gradually diminished. Eventually, it got to the point that I'd hit the panic button and pray simultaneously. We traveled on panic button and prayers, and God answered the prayers every time! Finally, it dawned on me that prayer was effective, and the panic button wasn't. That process took about two years! God is so patient with us!

POINTS TO PONDER

- Even when we're stuck in deep ravines, we can climb out.
- Deep ravine behaviors are fueled by intense fear, which manifests as fight, flight, or freeze.
- Growing in awareness and choosing to tackle one behavior at a time empowers us to overcome the fear that traps us.

For many reasons, not everyone is ready to leave their ditches. Because some are stuck and not ready to get unstuck, they may want to keep you in the mire too. Sometimes in order to get on the road, we need to exit a relationship. In the next chapter, we'll take a look at some things to consider when ditching people.

CHAPTER 7

DITCHING PEOPLE

"Making a big life change is pretty scary.
But know what's even scarier? Regret."
—Zig Ziglar

Sometimes we need to ditch the people and things that drag us down. That might be a spouse, parent, child, friend, relative, job, church, school, or organization. Some people or leaders in organizations overpower us, negatively influence us, bring out the worst in us, or interfere with our resolve to follow through with what we believe is right.

Knowing who and what to ditch and when can be challenging. We have become a nation quick to abandon or reject when things are not going our way. Or we have tried everything we know to get the other person to change to no avail, so we conclude they won't ever change. Then we give up on the relationship. While it is true that we have tried *everything we know to do*, that is *not* everything. Because we don't know what else to try and don't know where to go to learn about other options, it doesn't occur to us to look. This is why we come to believe we've tried everything. At least, that was my story.

As previously stated, I tried for many years to get my spouse to change, to no avail. When I finally started focusing on me and changing my actions, that changed our pattern of relating. It was difficult, but empowering!

From that, I learned there are much more effective ways of influencing change than the disempowering methods I had adopted from my family of origin. The new approaches existed outside the scope of my awareness until I got help and was presented with and became open to a new perspective.

With that as a backdrop, I want to talk about those situations in which leaving the relationship makes the most sense for all involved.

We *do* need to leave behind people or organizations that have strong negative influences on us. The Bible warns, "Don't fool yourselves. Bad friends will destroy you" (1 Cor. 15:33, CEV).

Discerning who and when to leave, examining all the options, and understanding the underlying motivation helps ensure the separation occurs for the right reason. Too often in our society, we dump the relationship just because we've run into difficulties. That's not necessarily cause to cut bait and quit fishing.

We are admonished in 2 Corinthians, "Don't become partners with those who reject God. How can you make a partnership out of right and wrong? That's not partnership; that's war. Is light best friends with dark? Does Christ go strolling with the Devil? Do trust and mistrust hold hands? Who would think of setting up pagan idols in God's holy Temple? But that is exactly what we are, each of us a temple in whom God lives" (6:14–18, MSG).

Here we receive guidance on the kinds of people to exclude from our inner circle. Their strong opinions will drag us down. They will give us no end of grief. No amount of your goodness will change their stance. However, strategic leaving of the relationship has the potential to positively influence the other person.

We can frame our exit speech in such a way that closes the door but leaves it unlocked if the other person decides to change and come back. An example of what that might look like is: "I see that we are at odds in the way we see things and neither of us is willing to change our stance. I care for you and want the best for you. Therefore, to protect both of us from hurting each other further, I'm going to break off our relationship. I know you might not think that is necessary, but from my perspective, I can't continue the way things have been going. If you ever change your mind or I change my mind, we can revisit this."

A friend's teenage daughter, Jenny, had a best friend, Jill, who started making bad choices. Disturbed by Jill's behavior, Jenny struggled to determine the best course of action. Finally, she decided that she could no longer be friends with Jill as long as Jill continued following that self-destructive path. Jenny informed Jill why she was ending the relationship and told her she'd be glad to be friends again if Jill ever decided to change her behavior. To Jenny's surprise, a few months later, Jill decided to change directions, apologized to her, and their friendship resumed!

SIGNS THAT IT'S TIME TO SAY GOODBYE—FOR GOOD OR FOR NOW

Those passages in first and second Corinthians provide some guidelines for the kind of people we should avoid or separate ourselves from.

1. Don't become partners with those who reject God

If you are a believer and your love interest is not, you will have additional challenges in your life. The same goes for a partner who *is* a believer but is not active in their faith. Your best option is to find someone who shares your level of involvement with your beliefs. It's so easy to settle for someone who is not fully on the same page as you in your convictions. Once the magic wears off, differences in levels of commitment to God can lead to contention.

If you're already married, some praying and fasting about this may be necessary to seek God's will in your situation. If your partner is an unbeliever, per 1 Corinthians 7:14, you influence your spouse in a positive way toward holiness, so the decision to stay or leave will depend on the specifics of your relationship.

2. Don't hang around bad people.

It's not that these people are *all* bad, just the part that blocks you from becoming the best version of you. What kind of bad company? If you tend to get drunk when hanging with others who drink, for you they are toxic. Even if they might not be getting drunk, if their behavior influences you to drink, and you feel powerless to stop once you get started, then your time would be more productively spent in the company of others.

Same thing applies if you have a massive sweet tooth. Don't apply to work in a candy shop. Working around sweets is not wrong, but if resisting the temptation overwhelms you, it's bad for you.

This logic also applies to people who do drugs, encourage infidelity, gamble, or engage in any other vice that drags you down.

3. Don't let others control you

If you feel controlled by another person's actions, not free to go where you want or be yourself, *and* you've given your best effort to crawl out of your own ditch but keep getting pushed back down, you may need to separate for a defined period of time for the purpose of working to improve the relationship. Sometimes having the space to learn how to develop and hold your own boundaries apart from the controlling or ditchy relationship is necessary.

Domineering people have forceful personalities. They are the type that will let you know what opinion you should have and what you should wear, think, or do. They are the ones who are always "right." Whole families, churches, communities, and nations can be like that.

On a national scale, for example, during World War II, Germans were "right." What Hitler said went. Because he used intimidation, force, extreme violence, and fear, people caved. They were justified in being fearful. Many people witnessed the death or torture of those who dared to take a stand. However, if all the passive people who secretly opposed Hitler had had the courage to stand on their beliefs and resist, he may not have succeeded. Perhaps the course of history would have been different. However, they didn't know *how* to resist in a way that would be effective. It required more energy and knowledge than the collective masses had at the time.

People with weaker convictions are swayed to go along with more dominant people. This is typical group behavior. In balance, it is good to have dominant people. They are leaders. Not everyone can be a leader or there would be no followers. To have harmonious relationships, it is necessary for members of groups to play various roles. When someone takes unfair advantage because of their role, oppression occurs.

This is the story of human history. It's been played out in every war throughout time. The dominant tribe, city, or nation exploits the weaker ones and often unjustly takes control of the conquered peoples' resources. That happened with Native American tribes when European immigrants came. Mexicans, Aztecs, Blacks, and

Israelites all met with the same fate. The conquerors make slaves out of the people or impoverish them through high taxes.

In families, this can also be true. One parent may be domineering, controlling, or verbally, emotionally, sexually, physically, or spiritually abusive, causing the rest of the family to either kowtow to their wishes or take severe punishment or banishment for refusing to comply. Out of fear, the weaker members of the family suffer in this kind of environment for years.

Children who are raised in such homes tend to repeat the pattern modeled for them. Conformity became mandatory for survival. By the time the child reaches adulthood, this behavior and way of relating has become ingrained. A victimized person often internalizes such lies, as: "I'm not worthy," "I'm not lovable," and "I deserve this (mistreatment)." In addition, common beliefs prevail: "I am trapped" and "there are no other options" (at least no other options seem viable). So, upon entering a romantic relationship, the only way the individual has learned to relate is replicated.

FISH OR CUT BAIT? I DECIDED TO KEEP FISHING

Most of the time, couples seek therapy only when they become desperate. Too often, by then they have reached the point of no return. It seems like some of my clients come to counseling just to obtain "proof" that the marriage or relationship is beyond repair.

The following scenario is typical: For years she has tried everything she knows to get him to change. She feels oppressed and powerless to make things better. Love has eroded to the point that she's finally ready to divorce. She issues an ultimatum, "Either go to see a counselor or I'm filing for divorce."

At that point, the partner *finally* begins to wake up to the reality that their relationship *might* have some issues. Mind you, she's been trying to tell him about the problems every way she knows how for the last five, ten, or twenty years! He reluctantly consents to therapy; she expects a 180-degree turnaround. He's still thinking *she's* the one that needs fixing. When progress in therapy is slow and arduous, calling it quits seems to be the best option. It appears obvious to the victim that the problems lie with the *mate*, especially if unfaithfulness, porn, drugs, alcohol, eating disorders, gambling, gaming, anger, intimidation, or any other glaring issue surfaces.

Sometimes these couples must separate or even divorce to interrupt unhealthy ways of relating. They need time to learn more effective skills to interact with one another in safety. Moving to separate bedrooms until they have gained traction may be helpful and economical. I know two sets of couples who divorced and were apart for several years. In the meantime, they worked on healing from the destructive familial patterns they had learned. Once they gained skills to interact in more effective ways, they repaired their relationships, got back together, and remarried.

On the surface, it seems the best way to fix a ditchy relationship would be to end it. At least, that's the consensus of most people in America. Me too. I wanted to end my marriage because I felt controlled, unable to be me, and unhappy. For a long time, the pathway out escaped me.

Then I learned from the "Rules for Being Human" that we are mirrors to each other.[1] At first, I vehemently denied that could be the case. Then, when I realized the behaviors I didn't like about my mate reflected aspects of myself that I disliked, I took that truth to heart, and began changing my actions. *That* got me started on my journey out of the ditch. I began examining what I could do differently instead of pointing out what he was doing to bug me. That was both challenging and empowering!

As the focus in my life shifted, I started standing up for what I wanted. Letting go of my role as master feather-smoother proved difficult, as I had been heavily invested in avoiding the anger of my spouse. Before the change, I stuffed down how I felt about situations because I worried that I'd upset him. I used to determine my actions based on how I *thought* he would react.

Changing our unhealthy relationship dynamic involved me taking the appropriate action despite the reaction I anticipated. *That* was hard! Feather smoothers like me want everyone around them to be calm, so deliberately choosing to allow someone to take responsibility for their own feelings—whether it be upset, angry, or disappointed with me—felt stressful.

Adjusting has been a long and rocky road. For over thirty-five years, I had invested in trying to convince *my spouse* to change because I believed he caused the problems, not me. Through counseling, support groups, step-studies, and reading lots of relationship books, I gained the necessary tools to begin my own transformation.

I can happily report that, now, life is amazing, for the most part!

I'm free to be me, while at the same time able to be considerate of others in my life.

As I write this chapter, I'm sitting on the balcony of a beautiful condo overhanging a 200-foot cliff facing the bay of San Carlos, Mexico. Prior to getting unstuck, I would have been on the dive boat with my husband doing something I enjoyed, but not pursuing my burning passion. With this change in how I do life, I'm watching sailboats lazily rock in the glass-smooth harbor, gazing on fascinating rock formations in the mountain across the bay, and appreciating spectacular Mexican architecture. I'm in my bathing suit, sipping on a cold brew, listening to my favorite music, while pursuing my dream to complete this book that I hope will help others. I'm free of feeling obligated to go on the boat just because my husband wants to dive. Watching an octopus explore his habitat while I snorkeled yesterday was fun, but in this moment, writing is more fun.

So, what does that have to do with ditching people?

DITCH THE DITCH

For a long time, I believed the only solution to my problem was ditching my husband. However, because I crawled out of my trench, it was like I threw him a rope to help him to crawl out of his. He grabbed on, and we both ditched our dysfunctional behaviors, not each other. I'm not going to lie; making the shift was *h-a-r-d!* But it was worth the effort; we ended up with a healthy relationship and intact family. So, changing how to do life is one option.

Because revamping one's own life is so difficult, the majority of people opt for ditching the relationship. A relative did that and now has a much happier situation with a second mate. People who learn from the mistakes in their first marriage and make some changes end up with happier second marriages. If they don't take time to evaluate their role in the failed relationship, the second marriage ends much like the first, and sometimes worse.

How does one discern whether it's best to end or work on healing the relationship? No cookie-cutter answers apply. Sorry. Many factors must be considered in determining the best course of action. Only God knows, so ask Him.

In the meantime, here are some questions to ask yourself:

"How Ditchy Are the Behaviors?"

If stuck in deep ravines, it might be necessary to leave. You can't improve much while living in terror of how your partner will react to every move you make. Interactions in those situations are way too toxic to come out safely. Read through the chapter on Deep Ravines; take a long, hard, honest look at what is happening in your relationship without minimizing, comparing, denying, or blocking it out. The depth to which an individual is stuck in their ditch is the degree to which the mate is stuck in powerlessness in the opposite extreme. For example, if one person is physically abusive, the mate shuts down and becomes a victim, living in flight or freeze mode. People need to crawl out of the ditches on both sides!

"What Are My Partner's Good Qualities?"

Yes, your partner also has good qualities. That's what drew you into the relationship and what keeps you there. Also, your life has been built around this person at some level, and if you have children, that complicates it in many ways. The positive attributes of a mate often get buried under all the negative experiences and hurtful events. To make the best decision, both positives and negatives must be weighed. However, for the sake of ending ditchy patterns, you may need to separate for a time, with a plan to reevaluate after six months, for example.

The member of the couple who recognizes the severity of the problems in the relationship often suggests to the other that counseling is necessary. Frequently, the partner is not willing to go, leaving the mate feeling stuck once again. Because the individual highlighting the issues believes the *partner* is the one in need of changing, when that person turns down the suggestion for therapy, it often doesn't occur to the distressed party that individual therapy could help the situation. Learning to relate differently will help *you*, whether you end up staying together or not. This also provides great practice in learning to speak up for what you want.

To end the stalemate, or stale relationship, the concerned party can announce, "Whether you decide to go or not, I'm going to get help with this relationship." Your mate's reaction provides you with valuable information to aid in determining which direction to go.

A separation gives space to work on healing your wounds so you can see clearly the best course of action. It also gives you time to see if your spouse is serious about making changes for their own sake, not just to win you back. Changes made with the goal of winning someone back usually don't turn out to be permanent. If that's the motivation, often after the partner returns, unhealthy patterns reemerge.

Let's back up to when you got into a relationship in the first place. List all your partner's good qualities.

We tend to draw someone into our lives who mirrors our childhood experience at some level. If you were loved (in a healthy way), had most of your needs met, and were cared for, you will find a mate who reflects those same qualities (give or take a few). Certain things my parents did I determined consciously to not allow in my life. Meanwhile, lots of other dysfunctional behaviors sneaked in under the radar.

My dad's temper connected to a short fuse. Lots of things could trigger it: doing something wrong, machinery breaking down, crops getting soaked instead of harvested, cows being stubborn, or Mom not making the kind of Jell-O he wanted. He mostly just yelled at us when those things happened, but I deeply desired for my dad to *not* be mad at me; therefore, I did what I could to win his approval and avoid upsetting him.

Fast forward to my late teens. Subconsciously, I looked for someone who wasn't trigger-happy angry and thought my husband-to-be was a lot different than my dad. While it is true that my husband didn't yell, he was manipulative and controlling in other ways. . .a little too much like my dad, but not enough for me to recognize the similarities. I didn't pick up on it until after we had been married for a while. What I couldn't see at the time was that I was responding to my husband just like I reacted to my dad, and I copied my mom's OF behaviors. Unwittingly, I helped recreate the patterns modeled by my parents.

Much later in life, I discovered that we tend to identify with one parent and marry someone who is more like the other. Of course, it's different enough to keep us from seeing the wheel go around again. We just play a variation on a theme. Until we become aware of what is going on and change, we repeat the pattern.

"What are my excuses for staying stuck in my ditch?"

At this juncture, I think it will help to have a look at some of the reasons we stay stuck in the ditch:

- **Deeply ingrained fear of failure**. If we try something and fail at it, somehow that spells doom for us. Could this be the hidden reason for staying stuck in the relationship and not seeking help? Aren't you glad Edison didn't give up after his 1,000th try? If he did, you'd be reading this book by candlelight.

- **Fear of being blamed for the demise of the relationship**. Terrified of being told, "You're responsible for this," I fell into this trap. Big time. That's why it took thirty years to figure out what I really wanted to do when I grew up. I was so afraid of making the wrong career decision. Guess what I did as a result? By default, without realizing it, I stayed stuck and took whatever jobs came my way.

- **Fear of what others will think.** Because I attended a church where divorce was not an option, I believed it was akin to turning my back on God. I feared God would reject me, worried about how others would view or judge me, and was afraid of being rejected by my church. It almost felt like it would be the end of the world if I divorced.

- **Financial dependence.** In the 1950s, my mom had five kids, two of them hemophiliacs needing frequent hospitalizations. Dad had good insurance with his factory job. Mom couldn't possibly support us kids on her own. Though tired of Dad's short temper, Mom lacked knowledge and resources to help her get out of the ditch, so she stayed and slowly wasted away inside until Alzheimer's gave her mind some relief from her sad, sad situation. Back then, resources to help her figure out how to improve her situation were nonexistent.

- **Emotional dependence.** Living in a strange town or not having many friends or relatives to provide support fosters unhealthy clinging to a mate. Even though it's as dysfunctional as a broken machine, it's familiar, and that seems better then complete isolation.

- **Waiting for the other person to change.** I believed all my problems stemmed from the way my spouse acted. My husband thought the problem was me. Most people seek therapy to learn how to get the *other* person to change. I tried every way I knew to point out things my spouse should do to improve, but, alas, he resisted every attempt I made to fix him.

- **Listening to the naysayers in your life**: Often people respond negatively to our dreams and aspirations because of fear or they were discouraged from pursuing theirs.

    Thankfully, when I wanted to quit my secure, well-paying government job to travel the country, my parents said, "You might as well do it while you're young." That was hands-down one of the best decisions I ever made in favor of something I really wanted to do. Thankfully, my husband was willing to follow my foolishness into the unknown for two and a half years. It was one of the biggest highlights of my adult life, one of the significant times when I had the courage to speak up. And it turned out to be a blessing for *both* of us.

- **Afraid to take action for fear of how others may react**. When telling ourselves, "I can't," we default to our ditch, allowing fear and powerlessness to keep us stuck. He may need you, be lost without you, or threaten to end his life if you leave, but how paralyzed do you feel? Your partner may be saying those things to emotionally manipulate you into staying or complying. Have you considered yourself and what you want in the mix? In my OF default, I forgot to consider me. I had no framework to consider myself *and* think of my spouse at the same time. While there are occasions to consciously choose to sacrifice time, resources, and skills in favor of the needs of others, it is important to consider your own wants and needs, also.

- **Feeling paralyzed**. See the bullet points above. Each one of these leave us feeling helpless, frustrated, and stuck! Powerless!

If we believed we were loved by the God who created us, and could trust His provision, we might just be able to step out of our tiny-ant existence into a much grander scene.

After identifying and evaluating the deep ravine behaviors we lived through in childhood, we may discover the pattern being replicated in some form in our current relationships. Only you know if the toxicity of your relationship rivals a plutonium waste site. If that's true, we may decide that time apart from the person who triggers our insecurities, low self-esteem, past pain, and desire to add arsenic to their meals is necessary. Leaving for a time may be the only way to gain the space to learn how we can do life. Differently. Better.

If that's the case, ditch that relationship! Perhaps temporarily. Maybe permanently. It may be the hardest thing you ever do. And the healthiest. It may just be the wake-up call your partner needs to realize their behavior is hurting them as much as it's hurting you. Then get to work on healing from your relational wounds, identifying the lies, fears, and negative beliefs that drove your ditchy behaviors and drew you into relationship with that scoundrel in the first place.

We tend to attract someone into our life who is at roughly the same emotional level we are. That may make you want to throw up because you see your mate as completely screwed up and here you are, Ms. Normal. At least, that's how I saw myself. I didn't see how wounded I was. If I am injured, so is my romantic partner. I just fail to see his wounds till I'm well into the relationship.

So, let's look at some of the patterns that emerge when one member of a couple comes to therapy:

- The client's efforts to improve spurs the significant other to get help too. That eventually happened with my husband and I, after I gave up trying to get him to change. Now our relationship is mostly balanced and healthy, though we both carry scars from the past.

- The person working on their healing advances emotionally to the point there is too much of a maturity gap between the two. The client gains the courage to end the relationship, continue their healing, and seek a healthier partner. The partner left in the dust often can't see their contribution and moves on to another unhealthy connection.

- The member of the couple who seeks help progresses a certain amount, which inspires their partner to get help. For example, a couple I'll call Sheila and Joe are struggling. Sheila goes to therapy, then Joe starts going too. He gets serious about his healing, while Sheila remains convinced it's all his problem. They separate. He grows more than she does, and she stays stuck somewhere in the ditch.

Most of the time I see the first two patterns.

Finally, let's talk about the benefits of getting help and sticking with the messed-up relationship you're in:

- I take my bags with me wherever I go, so I might as well unpack them before moving on. I was as screwed-up as my partner. I just couldn't see it. A new relationship may eliminate some of the current problems. However, some problems may be compounded, especially when children are involved.

- My partner is a mirror to me. In denial, I am unable to see how that could possibly be true. I think, "I'm OK, You're NOT." Clean off the mirror, look closely, and meditate on their behaviors for months if that's what is necessary to begin to see how their rude, crude, and socially unacceptable behavior reflects in your life. I was adamant that my husband's actions *in no way* reflected mine. When you change relationships, that new relationship is also a mirror. Changing mirrors doesn't change the image that is reflected.

- You become a positive influence for others. Your children, friends, relatives, co-workers and everyone in your life will see a model of what it looks like to do life differently. Better. Your raised energy level has a positive effect on every life you touch, whether directly or indirectly. You'll be amazed at the domino effect it sparks. I love Gandhi's statement: "We but mirror the world. All the tendencies present in the outer world are to be found in the world of our body. If we could change ourselves, the tendencies in the world would also change. As a man changes his own nature, so does the attitude of the world change towards him. This is the divine mystery supreme. A wonderful thing it is and the source of our happiness. We need not wait to see what others do."[2]

- Our children will appreciate our work. The only children who want their parents to separate are those who witness violence, or constant bickering. What they want then is the end of the fighting, not the end of the relationship. They would be delighted to have their parents learn how to get along! It's very stressful to children to have a front row seat at their parent's fight club.

- My kids have expressed appreciation numerous times for the work we've done to improve ourselves. We value seeking help to let go of hurtful habits and replace them with tools to work through conflict and problems. We model for our children listening to each other and honoring the other person. I love spending time with my kids and their families because we have done the hard work of learning to get along (James 3:17–18, MSG). If your family isn't at that place, know that you, too, can climb out of the deepest ravine to foster significantly better relationships.

When I change how I interact, the other person must respond differently, not out of coercion, but because my actions require a different response. Conversely, when we try to get them to change, they dig trenches of resistance, and then we feel frustrated and powerless. This has been my story most of my married life.

When thinking solely of the needs of the other, obligation, resentment, and disempowerment reign. When the focus centers on our own needs, we are demanding, angry, and disappointed. This explains the prevalence of ditches in our lives everywhere we look. When we love others and ourselves simultaneously, we model true, sacrificial love. That's easier said than done, but with God all things are possible.

Often couples justify a divorce because, "It is really hurtful for the kids to see us arguing all the time, throwing things, calling each other names, and slamming doors." Of course, it's hurtful for the kids to see that! In fact, it's traumatizing to them. *And* it's destructive to you too. When we're that stuck, it doesn't even occur to us that we could learn a new way to relate. Escape seems the only way. But we can develop healthy skills for listening, resolving conflict, honoring, and respecting each other.

POINTS TO PONDER

- There are occasions in which the best move is seeking separation for a time from a toxic relationship.
- It's important to evaluate all the reasons for your decision to select the best option for everyone involved.
- You may need to muster all the resources available to you to break the generational legacy of bad relationships.
- Once you decide to separate, let go of what you anticipate will happen.
- Plan to reevaluate in three or six months.
- Ultimately none of the good reasons for staying stuck in a deep ravine work in our favor.
- Take a close look at what is keeping you stuck, then develop a plan to start getting out and act on that.
- Unpacking your baggage will lead to a better life.
- You may need a professional baggage un-packer to help. It's worth it.
- Determining to change for the better in your current relationship is the healthiest and hardest thing you can do. But it comes with the biggest payoff, especially if you have kids, because they learn from your example, and they get to have both parents under one roof.
- Your choices may influence your partner to do their own healing work.

- The hardest part involves acting despite the anticipated reaction of the other party.
- Determine the best move, taking all people into consideration, including yourself, do it, and leave the results to God.

Freedom comes through empowerment—valuing your thoughts, feelings, concerns and desires equally with those of others.[3] That takes work and awareness of how your actions affect others and you. It's easy to learn these principles but will take months and years to master. It's worth it. Why not become the best person you can be and have the best relationships on the planet?

It's time for us to find a pathway to begin crawling out of our respective ditches!

CHAPTER 8

BUILDING A PATH OUT OF THE DITCH

"Not everything that is faced can be changed,
but nothing can be changed until it is faced."
—James Baldwin

For me to climb out of either ditch, I needed to start considering and valuing *my own* Thoughts, Feelings, Concerns, and Desires (TFCD), while simultaneously remembering my spouse's viewpoint.[1] I did not know how to do that! I could think of *me* in my MF ditch, and I could think of *him* in my OF ditch, but do both at the same time? Knowledge of how to find balance eluded me. No matter which extreme I lean towards, I need to value both of us equally! *How hard is that when we disagree?!*

Of course, I had no clue how to find the happy medium any more than I knew how to get out of my OF ditch or how I kept going from one ditch to the other!

Once I woke up, however, the pathway began to emerge. It started with noticing: identifying what I'm doing that needs to change and modifying my communication approach—how I say it, and the tone of voice I use. I discovered what kept me feeling powerless, when before I didn't even recognize that was how I felt inside, and that led me down the path to empowerment. In the process, I also learned better boundaries, which are necessary for healthy relationships.

Awareness is the first step of change. Unless we see our ditchy behaviors for what they are, recognize what triggers them, and understand what topics push, drive, or send us diving into the ditch, we are doomed to continue the patterns passed down from our ancestors.

Once alerted to where I was and what kept me stuck, I reached a turning point. I decided I didn't want to be there anymore! Just how to get out of the ditch had not yet become clear, but that determination was like turning on a flashlight, illuminating the next step.

Becoming aware takes time. After realizing how many ditch behaviors infiltrated my everyday life, I felt overwhelmed. Understanding the change process helped reduce that feeling and made it manageable.

WHAT CHANGE LOOKS LIKE

In forging a new path, my first challenge involved confronting my understanding of what the learning curve looked like. I had always assumed it was a gradual, smooth, upward movement, like a line starting on the ground and gradually sloping upward, like the right side of a skateboard half-pipe.

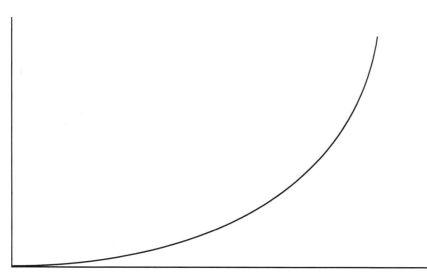

A workshop on interpreting transitions in American Sign Language (ASL) shattered that view. In that training, we started by interpreting a selection. Because I was a seasoned interpreter, that was easy. The instructor then explained some features of the language that were new to me. At the end we were instructed to interpret the same excerpt again, only this time incorporating our newly acquired knowledge. The second attempt was a disaster! I felt like a novice again. *What happened?*

I entered the workshop with existing knowledge of ways to shift from one thought to another. At the workshop, the new information on which signs to use to shift from one topic to the next entered short-term storage in my brain. When it came time to incorporate what I had just learned with knowledge stored in long-term memory, my brain couldn't cope. The new information had not yet become integrated into permanent storage, hence the breakdown in ability to skillfully interpret the exercise at the end of the workshop. Here's what I discovered:

We start with the sum total of what we know about a given topic.

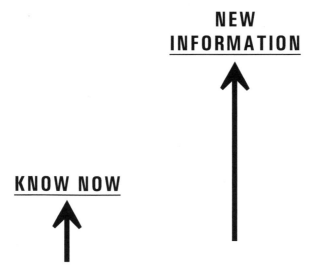

Then we gain new information. The graph now looks like this:

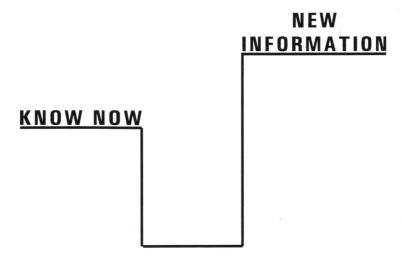

A lot happens before we complete integration of new knowledge. It's like our brain has to take down all the old scaffolding supporting our current bank of knowledge. Then we must

1. figure out what information needs to be added to what we already know,

2. filter out what must be deleted because the new makes the old obsolete,

3. sort out what gets modified when some of the old is still valid but some aspect has changed, and

4. learn what stays the same.

That's a lot for our brains to process, and it takes time. This is what it looks like:

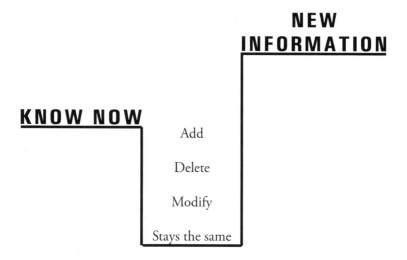

No matter the topic—whether it's getting used to a new job, acquiring a new skill, or changing the manner in which we relate to others—our brains go through the same process. Because of that, the learning "curve" starts to looks more like sideways bleachers than the smooth curve I once envisioned.

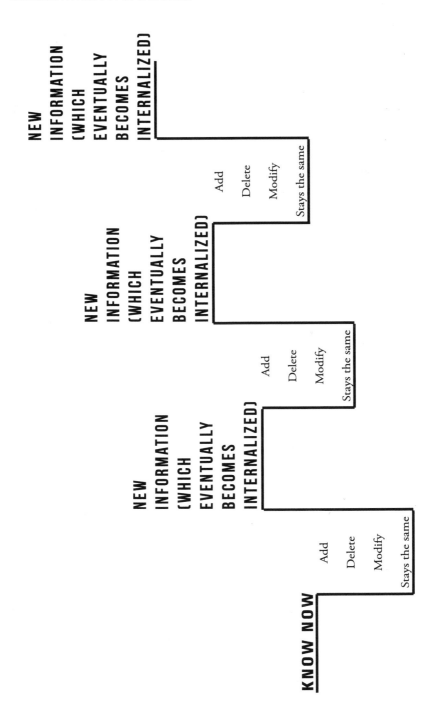

The second point about change relates to *how* it happens. I've always wanted others to change immediately, make a 180-degree about-face, be consistent, and have it internalized *yesterday*. However, *I* can't live up to that standard, even though that's what I want from others, especially my mate. No one can change established patterns at the drop of a hat. Expecting to change a lifelong habit in a short time frame leads to discouragement and quitting before you get started. Notice any extreme with that kind of expectation?

Have you or someone you know ever started a diet, expected to be 100 percent consistent with the new regime, gotten discouraged after day three because the scales refused to budge, and then quit? That's our subconscious expectation rearing its unrealistic head.

A luxury ocean liner getting ready to leave port provides a much more accurate picture of the process of change. If you've been on a cruise, perhaps you stood at the railing and watched as the crew members prepared the ship to leave port. The engineer fires up the engines. You can feel the vibration reverberating through the ship long before the crew weighs anchor. Then, the anchor is raised and ropes securing the ship to the dock are uncoiled and returned to their resting place onboard. After the ship gains freedom from its moorings, it inches away from the dock.

At first, the movement is imperceptible. A sliver of light slices between the dock and the ship, prying the two apart. Slowly, the wedge between them grows. Finally, the ship gains sufficient separation for the tugboat to intervene, coax it around, and nudge it into open waters where it is able to slowly increase speed, eventually acquiring enough independence to continue under its own power.

The tugboat helps turn the ship turn around, guides it through the narrow harbor, and stays with it until it's safely out of danger in open waters.

That's exactly how change happens for us. It starts with a thought. That's like starting the engines. You are introduced to a new idea and start to think about it. Nothing perceptible happens externally. Sometimes we ponder a new thought, idea, approach, or action for a long time before deciding to take action. The engines are running, but the boat isn't going anywhere. . .yet.

After considering a new concept and evaluating its merits and demerits, an individual decides to take a small step in the direction of change. Everything must be ready before the ship begins to move. At first, movement is tentative. Attempts at new ways are made, but patterns predominate. The old way is so automatic! The new takes such conscious effort! The ship inches away from the dock.

Determined steps propel us toward the forging of new habits, and the grip of old patterns loosens as we head in the new direction. The ship moves far enough away from the dock to begin to turn around.

To break old habits, we seek God in prayer, enlist the help of others, and get input from friends and relatives we trust. Perhaps we turn to a pastor, mentor, or counselor for guidance. The tugboat nudges the ship in a new direction.

With determination, commitment, and the power of God, change takes root and becomes established. We notice that it is easier to engage our new thoughts and actions. Old ways diminish and begin to fall away. The ship heads toward open waters.

Deciding to do something different, accepting that it is a process, and choosing to keep at it rather than give up leads to success, and eventually, we experience deep satisfaction. Big change happens in tiny increments.

Working on one issue at a time feels manageable; whereas it is overwhelming to attempt to overcome several ditch behaviors at the same time. Starting with one thing helps us gain traction. Changing even one reaction is freeing! Once we successfully crawl out of the ditch in one area, it becomes a little easier to tackle the next one. Over time, momentum grows.

Break down the process into small, manageable chunks, and allow two weeks to a month to just notice how frequently a particular ditch behavior manifests. This helps us avoid the tendency to be self-critical.

Suppose you tend to be sarcastic. When your relationship is going well, making a sarcastic remark in fun may seem harmless enough. However, usually there's a barb of some sort masking hurt, resentment, or anger, and the comment carries a bitter, demeaning, or mocking tone. Notice what topics and which people prompt those kinds of remarks to slip out. What feelings drive that? This is the information-gathering phase, where awareness grows of where and how frequently a behavior pops up. Work on changing the reaction comes next.

Also notice when others are sarcastic towards you. What's going on in the relationship? Do you feel "off" or have an uneasy feeling about the interaction but can't quite name it? What others do to us is outside our control, but we can begin to identify and express how we feel about it. Consider what happened just prior to that hurtful interaction. Perhaps something was said or done that the other person took the wrong way? Becoming more alert to our own ways of interacting and noticing how that contributes to the reactions of others provides valuable insight.

Instead of owning my experience and saying, "I'm feeling pressured by you," my tendency is to accuse: "You are pressuring me." But when I describe how I *feel* by labeling what *you are doing*, I unwittingly render myself the powerless victim. I feel controlled by how another's actions impact me.

This age-old way of interacting prevents both parties from identifying their feelings and the reaction stemming from them. Both feel powerless to change it because neither one sees their part in the situation. By identifying and expressing how *we* are affected by *each other* in the moment, we serve others and ourselves better.

It's not easy to do, especially for OFs. At times it's hard for me to figure out how *I* feel. It may require time to ponder or journal to discover deeply buried emotions. Then, after understanding what our feelings tell us, consider options and come up with possible replacement words or behaviors beforehand to help speed up the process of change. It helps to engage family members. Find out from family members how they'd rather have a request or question approached.

Enlist someone to help point out the targeted word or behavior you desire to eliminate. Figure out *how* you want them to point it out in a manner that is not irritating to you. Accepting the fact that I'm doing something ditchy is difficult enough without someone exposing it in a grating way.

All this *thinking*—about how you say what you say and considering how others may be impacted and react to you, even if nothing happens externally—*is change*. Before the behavior was brought to your attention, it wasn't even on your radar!

"I thought about doing it differently, but only did it once this week." That's one more time than you did it the week before! Only look at successes and applaud yourself for even tiny improvements. You might even keep a calendar on your phone to mark every time you remember to do your target action. When you do that, you will feel good about the change you are making instead of beating yourself up for not doing it perfectly the first, second, or umpteenth time.

Now that we have built a pathway, let's see what it looks like to begin crawling out of our ditches.

POINTS TO PONDER:

- The change process looks like sideways bleachers.
- Big change happens in tiny increments.
- Focus on changing one thing at a time.

CHAPTER 9

STEPPINGSTONES FOR CRAWLING OUT OF THE DITCH

"Be who you are and say what you feel, because those who matter don't mind and those who mind don't matter."
—Dr. Seuss

Now that we know crawling out of the ditch is going to take some time, effort, and a lot of patience, we can shift our attention to the steps that will help us get out and stay out.

There are two foundational initial steps: "noticing" and "modifying communication."

Noticing consists of:

- taking note of what topic you're discussing when the worst ditch behaviors emerge,
- the ditch you're in,
- your default behaviors,
- your partner's ditch and default behaviors, and
- the fears driving these destructive patterns.

Modifying our communication consists of rewording how we start conversations, adjusting our tone of voice, and changing how questions and statements are formed.

Let's take a closer look at each of these elements.

NOTICING

The Topic

Neither my husband nor I had a clue how to navigate a situation when we strongly disagreed. No wonder we often landed in the ditch!

When finding an amicable solution seemed impossible, we headed straight toward our ditchy default behaviors. The negative feelings piled up over time, causing distancing.

My Ditch and Behavior

Once I've identified the topic that sends me to a ditch, it helps to know in which extreme I got stuck, because then I know who I need to remember to take into consideration. When I go to the OF ditch, I need to think about what I want.

Habitually used to giving up what I want, I find it challenging to consider myself. For example, on a recent visit to Las Vegas, I wanted to see a couple shows. Three or four performances sounded appealing, but a cold influenced my energy levels. My husband got up super early every day and had several miles of walking under his belt before I even began to stir. Therefore, by the time 8 p.m. rolled around, he was ready to crash. I found it impossible to strongly advocate for the shows I wanted to see because he wasn't interested, and I didn't feel well. We ended up not going to any shows. I observed it was easy to give up something I wanted to do because he wasn't interested. And it was equally difficult to discern whether it had more to do with me not feeling well or if it was habit to not pursue my own interests. I think it may have been equal parts of both. I reacted passively.

When I'm in my MF ditch, I'm adamant about doing what I want without giving thought to how it impacts others. If that's where I've landed, I'm reminded to consider the rest of my family in my decision-making process.

When I decided to pursue a counseling degree, I gave some thought to how the family would be impacted and went part-time instead of full-time. However, I couldn't figure out how to balance everyone's needs, so I just avoided thinking about it. My schooling had a major financial and time impact on our family. In this case I acted selfishly. If I had it to do over again, getting input from everyone and discussing options would have helped us all.

My Partner's Ditch and Behavior

Chances are you'll find your partner in the opposite ditch from the one you're in. Often, it's much easier to notice what the other person is doing than it is to see our own ditchiness. From my perspective, he's the one with the beam in his eye, not me, though Matthew 7:3 would suggest otherwise. When I stop and think about how his behavior triggers me, I can then do something about it. Often, a clear conversation can short circuit an old reaction.

Also, take note of how the other person reacts to how you say or do things, especially when it is undesirable. What did they do that influenced your actions? Note how they sent you to your ditch. What reaction do you pull from your repertoire? This awareness speeds the process of change.

Underlying Fears

Remember that the fears driving our ditchy behaviors may be difficult to identify. However, this is the key to being set free. Naming the fear helps point to what can be done to eliminate it. Figure out how to handle the fear and take action. We'll discuss what to do about fear in Chapter 16.

The communication approach—meaning *how* wants and needs get expressed—requires some modifications if we have been taught to approach a topic in an indirect way, if the tone is manipulative, forceful, demanding, or if statements and questions are disempowering in the way they are constructed.

MODIFYING COMMUNICATION

Conversation Startups

My conversation startups kept me feeling powerless (when I didn't even recognize that's how I felt). Learning a new way to communicate is empowering, though it has been as challenging as learning a whole new language! Copying the way my parents spoke was so automatic. I didn't have to think about it. Words just fell out of my mouth and landed me in the ditch.

The way we start a conversation impacts interactions. If you greet your spouse at the door with a question like, "Did you do the errand I asked you to do?" perhaps you will get a "Yes" back, but it might make your partner feel resentful and think that you only care about what they can do for you, when that wasn't your intent at all. Your mate then reacts to the feeling he experienced after that thought, attacks back, and suddenly you're in an argument and have no idea what started it. You don't think you had anything to do with his reaction. You think he must have come home in a grumpy mood and blame him for the conversation turning sour. Meanwhile, he's thinking the same thing about you. Both feel justified in their reactions and never stop to consider that the communication start-up pattern played a significant role. If hubby's first words upon arrival home are "What's for dinner?" that might evoke the same downhill spiral for you.

Therefore, starting a conversation with, "Hello!" "Welcome home!" "How was your day?" or "What was your high and low today?" reminds your partner that you value him or her as an individual first and that you want to know what's happening in their world before you launch into what you want from them.

Another shift in start-ups involves providing a heads-up about a discussion. Instead of diving right in, now I begin with: "I was thinking about (the topic) and would like to have a conversation with you about that. I'd like to schedule a time to talk about it."[1] While it may sound like you're about to schedule a business meeting, allowing your spouse time to consider your ideas before discussing them works in your favor, especially if you have an MF spouse whose automatic answer tends to be "No!" Allowing your partner some time to think about it prevents them from feeling caught off guard. I've gotten a lot more yeses simply from changing my approach. Our discussions have been a lot more enjoyable, too.

Another way my communication start-ups often landed me in the ditch had to do with how I approached discussing what I wanted to do or get. Starting with, "Do you think I could get X?" gave away all my power without my realizing it. I asked for permission for something as though still a child. Because my husband's initial default answer to any question tended to be no, that's what I'd get, especially if it was about something uninteresting to him. Since he said no, I felt like I'd been stopped in my tracks, unable to move forward to pursue what I really wanted.

Instead, now I start with "I would like X. Are you interested?" Or if I want something, I change it to a comment: "I'm planning to get this item." With that kind of wording, the outcome is completely different. If he says no, I'm free to seek other avenues. It also helps him because he clearly knows what I want. I've learned that he desires to please me a lot more than I thought. I just wish I would have known about our default tendencies a lot sooner! We could have avoided much hurt, disappointment, missed opportunities, and arguments. Our approach to any given topic impacts how it is received, influences the interaction, and often the outcome.

Tone of Voice

The second aspect of improving communication relates to how words sound to others. Unbeknownst to me, my vocal quality often grated on my husband like nails on a chalkboard. I couldn't understand how that could be true. My tone didn't sound bad to *me.*

But then, my spouse also denied how *his* tone bothered me. We've had more than a few arguments about whether the other had a "tone" when saying something. As I write this, that sounds silly, but I can guarantee neither of us thought so at the time. As difficult as it was for both of us to accept, we finally agreed that each other's perspective is valid instead of arguing, justifying, and denying that our comments came with "an attitude." It just goes to show how negative feelings leak out through our inflection, even when they are hidden from ourselves!

Ensuring that we have a positive or neutral spirit also affects successful communication. We must rely on feedback from others to shift how our words sound to them. Our interactions with others improve when we are receptive to other people's assessments of how we come across to them and are willing to work on improving. The payoff results in more harmonious relationships.

The Way Questions and Statements are Formed

The third aspect impeding successful communication involves word choice, such as asking for permission when a statement is more fitting. Without realizing it, I spoke in indirect ways instead of being direct. Which sounds better to you? "Do you think you can bring home some milk?" or "I'd like you to pick up some milk." The way the first example is phrased calls the individual's ability into question.

Often, a request was approached in the negative, almost implying that I didn't expect to get what I desired. "Why don't we go hiking today?" as if I'm asking for all the reasons why we should avoid exercise. "You can't go out to play until you get your room cleaned." Instead of that statement providing impetus for the kid to get his room done, it often had the opposite effect. The child would give up in defeat, believing that getting done in time to play was beyond his reach. "You don't think we could go on a trip, do you?" Talk about a negative way to approach something I wanted to do! Because of fear of rejection and pattern of not getting what I wanted, I believed that framing my requests in these ways hedged against anticipated disappointment. However, the negative way I approached things pulled into my life the very things I feared!

My first significant effort to change the manner in which I approached interactions involved eliminating the phrases "you should" and "you should've." I grew up in a "you should've" household. My parents, especially my dad, frequently told us what we *should* have done. I'm sure that's what he heard from his parents too. His intention was for us to learn from those experiences and do things differently in the future. However, it resulted in me feeling powerless. I could not change what I had already done, and it didn't occur to me to translate that to "Think about how you can approach a similar situation in the future in a better way."

William Backus's *Telling Each Other the Truth* revealed to that "should" is problematic because it conveys an obligation. "Need, should, ought, or have to"—triggers the rebellious little kid inside that says no to everything. We don't like to be told what to do.

Furthermore, because we heard those words so much growing up, they became cemented into our vocabulary as adults. We copy the speech patterns of our parents: how they approach a topic, the way they put words together, their directness (or lack thereof), tone, emotional expression, and a host of other subtleties in communication. I never once considered the feelings of powerlessness I regularly experienced because of those factors, nor did I understand the influence those manners of speaking had over communication outcomes.

In our household, we 'should-ed' on each other all the time. It was such a common phrase for us. Little did we know, living under that pile of "should" stunk!

When I decided to eliminate the phrase "you should" from my vocabulary, I asked my husband to help me by pointing out when those words slipped out of my mouth. The phrase was so ingrained that I didn't even hear myself say it! It took several months to change that habit.

My point: the way we put words together impacts how others receive them, and our habits are so automatic that we don't even know we're repeating them.

Have you ever heard someone say, "You should see that movie"? It's intended to be positive and encouraging. What we mean by that most of the time could more accurately be expressed as, "I really liked that movie, and knowing you, I think you'd like it too." Reread those two examples and notice the difference in your internal reaction.

Changing how I approached a conversation, the tone used, and my word choice turned out to be the tip of the iceberg!

We needed a framework of safety for communicating, where both of us could share our perspective, opinions, concerns, wishes, and emotions in a cooperative atmosphere, and we didn't have that. I too easily felt overpowered by my husband's direct approach and tended to shut down, while he got frustrated with my oblique methods. Neither of us knew how to say what we felt without the other feeling attacked or put down in some way.

We both needed to hear, to feel heard, and to understand the other's perspective, especially when we disagreed. Neither of us knew how to listen to complaints from the other, and neither did we know how to discuss concerns without both of us becoming triggered and defensive. That blocked us from being able to discuss critical topics in order to reach an amicable solution. No instruction for executing effective dialogues was provided at home or in school.

No wonder knowledge of how to address conflict without escalating into an argument is missing in most relationships!

POINTS TO PONDER:

When ditch behaviors emerge
- Notice the topic
- The ditch you're in
- Your default behaviors
- Your partner's ditch
- Your mate's default behaviors
- The fears driving the actions

Modify communication
- Change conversation start-ups
- Attend to tone of voice
- Notice the way questions and statements are formed

CHAPTER 10

THE ABCDs OF NEGATIVE INTERACTIONS

"Now I know my ABCs.
Next time won't you sing with me?"
—Charles Bradlee

*I*n a graduate school class on marital and premarital counseling, we were required to investigate fourteen approaches to couples' therapy. Empirical research proved that one method stood head and shoulders above the rest.

The approach that promised the greatest long-term results was something called Relationship Enhancement (RE).[1] Trying it out personally seemed like a no-brainer to me. I figured that if this method could improve the communication difficulties in our marriage of over three decades, it could help *anyone*. So, my husband and I signed up to attend the two-day workshop.

In addition to the life-changing skills we learned, we also discovered we should not attack, criticize, or blame. Nodding like bobble-heads, we agreed to work on that. Criticizing and blaming seemed obvious, but to be honest, I didn't believe I was attacking; I just knew when others verbally attacked me.

Over the years, I developed ways to help people—clients as well as my husband and myself—recognize and address some of these behaviors.

One day I was working with a client who was lamenting the intolerable actions of others when the idea popped into my head to lay out for her what was really happening in her life. I listed attacking, blaming, criticizing, and defending, in a column. The first time I wrote these ABCDs on the whiteboard, I was dumbfounded at what I discovered!

Before I tell you my revelation, let me summarize for you what I spelled out for my client:

Attacking or accusing occurs when:
1. *We tell, suggest, or hint at what someone did or should do.* We know we are doing this when we use phrases like, "*You* should, ought, have to, must, or need to. . ." "If *you* just. . ." "Why don't *you*. . .""If I were *you*, I would. . ."

2. *We engage in name-calling or labeling someone's behavior.* We know we are doing this when we use phrases like: "You are irritating." "You are rude." "You are too pushy." "Sissy!"

3. *We tell someone what they did to us.* We know we are doing this when we use phrases like: "*You* hurt my feelings." "*You* disappointed me." "*You* made me mad."

4. *Our tone or attitude is sarcastic, irate, irritated, angry, annoyed, mocking, or demeaning.* We know we are doing this when we say things like: "Well, *it's about time* you showed up!" "There you go, again!" "I should have known I couldn't depend on you."

<u>B</u>laming occurs when:

1. ***We assign all the blame to the other person.*** We know we are doing this when we use phrases like: "It's all your fault." "This wouldn't have happened if you hadn't done that."

<u>C</u>riticizing occurs when:

1. ***We point out the faults, flaws, and failures of others.*** We know we are doing this when we use phrases like: "You did that wrong." "Why didn't you take out the trash?" "Your hair is a mess."

<u>D</u>efending or deflecting occurs when:

1. ***We defend ourselves by refusing to share any responsibility.*** We know we are doing this when we use phrases like: "You didn't tell me I was supposed to do that!" "It's not my fault that the door got left open." "You didn't speak loud enough."

2. ***We deflect attacks, accusations, blame, or criticism by attacking, accusing, criticizing, or blaming right back.*** We know we are doing this when we use phrases like: "Well, **you** didn't do what you were supposed to, either!" "It's **your** fault for leaving the door opened!" "**You** didn't listen to me when I told you."

WHEN YOU SEE THE COMMON DENOMINATOR, YOU'LL UNDERSTAND WHY YOU FEEL POWERLESS

As I mapped out these negative responses for my client, something stuck me—hard.

Every single one of these responses has a common denominator. And when you see it, you'll soon discover why attacking, accusing, blaming, criticizing, defending, and deflecting doesn't make you feel any better. In fact, engaging in these forms of communication can leave you feeling even more vulnerable and powerless than before!

Here's why:

When we engage in these forms of communication, we are abdicating our emotional well-being to another person.

If we are attacking or accusing, who are we asking to change? *The other person.*

If we blame a problem on someone else's bad behavior, who are we waiting to fix the problem? *The other person.*

If we are pointing out another person's faults, flaws, or failures, who needs to change? *The other person.*

When we defend, who do we need to acknowledge our blameless state? *The other person.* And when we deflect, who do we need to back off? *The other person.*

Are you noticing a pattern?

In each case, when we attack, accuse, blame, criticize, defend, or deflect, we are waiting on the *other person* to do something to solve the problem. How are we left feeling? Frustrated, powerless, and helpless!

Wow!

That was the house in which I grew up. *That* was how my parents talked. They expressed how they felt by labeling others and describing others' actions.

Instead of saying, "I feel irritated," they'd say, "You are irritating me."

When I felt upset, they'd ask, "What's wrong with you?"

I copied that communication pattern and replicated it in my relationships, too. I spent most of my life feeling powerless and didn't even know it!

Since this discovery, I've also learned how common it is in many, if not most, households. Notice the dialogue in your favorite TV shows, particularly when an argument starts and escalates. Notice how attacks, accusations, blame, criticism, defensiveness, and deflection fuel the fire. Every escalating argument consists of those elements.

Our assessment of what the other person needs to do, what they are doing, and how their actions affect us may be 100 percent accurate! But, if our focus is concentrated on the other person, we get stuck in *powerlessness*.

Let's explore the ABCDs at a deeper level to understand what's going on behind the scenes.

Attack/Accuse

If we are getting along well, we tend not to mind someone else giving us direction. However, if our partner, parents, kids, or peers are being testy and aren't in a very cooperative mood, ordering them around doesn't go over very well. Therefore, approaching the situation with "you should" becomes triggering and results in a defensive or angry reaction.

Mind you, when I'm the one explaining what needs to be done, describing another person's behavior, or giving orders, it doesn't *feel* to me like I'm attacking. I'm just telling it like it is or explaining what needs to be done. At least, that's my perspective. I *think* I'm communicating what I want and letting the other person know how I feel. When I do this, I believe I'm expressing my desires clearly. Also, most of the time, I think I'm saying it in a nice way.

If you say, "You can stay at my house and spend time with our dog while I'm gone," that sounds harmless enough, but the well-intentioned suggestion could be met with a defensive response because the recipients may feel like they're being told what to do or assume you just want them to watch your dog, even if that's not your intent at all.

When I was young and sharing an apartment with a roommate, I often said, "You can do X if you want." After a week or two hearing me make those offers, she shot an angry retort at me: "I don't need permission from you to do what I want!" I thought I was saying things in the politest way I knew; I didn't realize it was a form of telling her what to do. Back then, I didn't know my ABCDs.

Of course, even if I do not think I'm attacking at all, the person on the receiving end can have quite a different experience. Defensive reactions are a dead giveaway that my approach feels attacking to them.

My husband and I have gone around the merry-go-round of defensiveness more times than I can count. He would tell me: "You are attacking me." (Yep, that's an attack back; he's telling me what *I'm* doing.) In denial I'd reply, "No, I'm not. I'm just telling you how I feel."

Just as often, I felt attacked by him. Until I learned my ABCDs, I didn't even realize we engaged in this craziness, and I for sure didn't know how to end the cycle. It took acknowledging that his perception was as valid as mine (that was difficult), then figuring out what words make it feel like an attack to him, and identifying what feels like an attack for me.

There *is* a place for telling others what we want them to do. Tasks need to be completed, and we need to let others know when we need help. Often, just tweaking how we express the request will garner a more favorable response. Of course, it's important to ask in a polite way and say please. Switching from "you" to "I would like," "I prefer," "I need," "I want," changes it from telling someone what to do to letting them know what you want to happen. Offering options such as "if you choose," "if you are willing," "an option is," or "if you decide" makes it clear the other person has a choice.

If stating directly what you want sounds uncomfortable, consider which way you'd prefer. Would you rather have someone say, "You need to do that" or "I would like you to do that"?

The first comes across as an obligation, and if I refuse to do it, I'm rebelling. The second comes across as a request, and I have a choice to say, "I don't want to." We then can discuss other options if that's the response.

Also, as discussed in the previous chapter, the way the person on the receiving end responds has a lot to do with the tone, inflection, and attitude with which we say it. People pick up on fear, manipulation, condescension, and belligerence quickly, and they become resistant or passive aggressive in reaction.

Some have asked, "How will this tweaking help?" They counter, "I asked in a direct way for what I wanted." Often, it's just one or two words that spurs a defensive response. Take time to discover what words evoke negative reactions from the people in your life.

When the relationship isn't going so well, we tend to get stuck when the other person *doesn't* do what we've told them to do. The challenge lies in sorting out when it is appropriate to ask or tell others what to do and when it's not. It is also difficult to figure out how to express our desires in a different way than the method with which we're accustomed.

Our onslaught is not limited just to others. We can be just as guilty of attacking or labeling ourselves: "There I go again!" "I'm just not good enough." "She's prettier than I am." "I have to be perfect." "Nobody loves me." It's as important to recognize when we attack *ourselves* as it is to recognize when we do it to others. It's common, everyday behavior that we may have picked up from the adults in our lives that seems "normal." We tell ourselves "everybody does it" and "that's just the way life is." That may be true, but it doesn't have to continue to be that way. I want to establish a better, healthier way of living. Working on eliminating those self-deprecating, internal barrages benefits us and everyone around us. We judge others to the same degree we judge ourselves. It's not healthy, nor does it lead to a happy life. Plus, Jesus said not to judge (Matthew 7:1, KJV).

As parents raising children, it is even more challenging to discern when to tell a child what to do and when to say it in a different way. Many times a day, we need to issue commands to our kids. We get stuck when our little darlings don't do what we say. We resort to a more forceful tone, amp up the volume, add gestures, snap our fingers, point, do The Hokey Pokey and turn ourselves around all in an attempt to get our children to comply with our requests. In that moment, we feel powerless, whether we are consciously aware of it or not. We hit a dead end and don't know where to go from there. At least, I didn't.

The second form of attack involves labeling behavior: "You are lazy." "You are being rude!" "You never listen." "You don't care about me!" We describe how we see another person through labeling, and our estimation might even be accurate! I think I'm communicating what I feel, but I'm not doing it effectively or in a way that prevents the other person from feeling defensive.

Telling others what they should, ought, need, or have to do and labeling their behavior *feels* like an affront when I'm on the receiving end, though it doesn't when I'm on the one talking. When others do it to me, I definitely feel attacked! However, I could not identify it as such before I learned my ABCDs! We get triggered when told what to do. Could it be because we all hated it when we were kids?

Naming the words that became the spears in my heart opened my eyes to what caused me to feel attacked. Once I realized how those words affected me, I gradually became sensitive to words I employed that wounded those I love. I wish I could say I'm beyond saying hurtful things, but even when I have the best intentions, I still say things that occasionally offend others.

When I first went to a counselor, I couldn't name a feeling to save my life. I had not been taught to be in touch with my feelings, but rather to describe what I saw in others. I was great at making a statement or labeling; I was lousy at knowing how I felt about it. It was easy to say to someone, "You are proud and arrogant!" It was almost impossible to identify the underlying feeling of fear that I don't matter as much to the other person as they matter to me. I hid my feelings so well that I didn't know where I put them, how to find them, or how to go about expressing them.

When I say someone is rude or crude, I think I'm just telling it like I see it. True. But to the other it feels like I sent a pack of dogs charging at them. How do I change it from being an attack to a productive form of communication? That's in the next chapter.

Enough about attacking and accusing. Now let's take a closer look at blame.

BLAME

Blame is rampant in our world. It is one of the first defense strategies mentioned in recorded human history. God wanted to know how Adam and Eve found out they were naked. Adam promptly blamed Eve and God in one fell swoop: "The woman whom *you* gave to be with me, she gave me fruit of the tree, and I ate" (Genesis 3:12, ESV, emphasis added). Eve then passed the buck to the serpent. Ever since, the world has been playing the blame game. I got blamed, and I blamed my spouse and kids.

When stuck in a ditch, I could not see my part. Period. I only saw what my spouse did that hurt me. I blamed him fully. That left me frustrated and powerless, waiting for him to do something about it.

Once I took a hard look at the part I played, my life improved significantly because I was no longer powerless. First, in all situations, we have some ownership, even if it's passive. For example, when I'm standing in line and the person in front of me turns and accidentally elbows me, what is my piece? I stood too close.

Now, suppose I'm standing in line again, but this time it's at an event center. People crowd all around me, and I can't help being too close to the person in front of me. That individual turns and elbows me. Now, whose fault is it? I'm still too close to the person in front of me, so that's my part. However, now a lot of other people are also involved because they all crowded in too close. I still need to recognize my part while noting how others influenced what took place helps me not feel so alone in my mistake.

The factors influencing our actions compare to being surrounded by the masses waiting to get in at a concert venue. We internalize a variety of lies we believe to be true, and then live accordingly. Hurting others stems from that. Our mistakes and misbehaviors are predicated on our parents and how each one affected us. Our generational line and what our paternal and maternal sides passed down to us influenced us as well. Then our siblings, friends, neighbors, church, pastors, teachers, other students, coaches, groups with whom we were involved, events, work, the media, and world events all play a role. The list goes on. We are impacted in so many ways by so many people, it's like the crowd is pushing in on every side. Then there is our own unique reaction to those experiences; *that's our responsibility*. When I see mistakes through that lens, it's much easier to admit my faults, and to be more forgiving of others. Sometimes my piece is small; other times I'm guilty of the lion's share of the issue. When I practice taking ownership for relatively minor things, it becomes easier to own up to my major mistakes.

For instance, if I have been hurt over and over by people I care about, I might conclude that people are out to get me. I then believe that is true. Then every time something goes wrong, I think it was done intentionally. While that may be true occasionally, it is not true most of the time. But you could not convince me otherwise because I'm locked into the falsity, which I'm sure is true. Blaming and ascribing evil motivations to others keeps me a victim.

My dad grew up in a home where he was ridiculed and shamed for making mistakes. He learned his lesson well: *Don't admit to any errors.* Because he was blamed for things he didn't do, he reacted the same way with his kids. We got blamed for anything that went wrong. The shame of being at fault for something was unbearable for him. It was for me, too.

All people have done things for which they feel ashamed. We are all guilty of wrongdoing. The more we try to hide our shame and guilt, pretending we're fine, the more it wreaks havoc in our lives. It causes us to behave in ways that bring on even more shame and guilt. If you don't believe me, verify that with any addict.

I learned to take responsibility for what *wasn't* mine. Then I hid, lied, denied, or did whatever I could to avoid blame when

I *was* at fault, just like my dad did. That left me feeling stuck. I couldn't do anything about the errors I *didn't* make and turned a blind eye to my own faults. That prevented me from correcting the problem, and I just tried to run away from it.

When I take all the blame, believing it's *all* my fault, that sends me into depression. Plus, when I do that, I play victim, which I've done countless times in my life. It's a wonder I'm not dead with as many times as I've played martyr! As a mom, a lot of times, I felt like my children's issues were all my fault. While I was responsible for some of it, other factors played a role as well, as we've already discussed.

The way my kids turned out was not all on me. By the way, they turned out amazing! I can't take all the credit for that, either. Lots of great people influenced the men of character my sons became. I just played a part—sometimes for better, sometimes for worse.

CRITICIZE

When we criticize, focus centers on the other person and what is wrong, faulty, or flawed.

The tendency to be judgmental of our children, ourselves, and others is widespread throughout the world and has been passed down for generations. We often feel like others are judging us; that's because internally we are critical of ourselves, others, or both. Jesus said if we want to be free of feeling judged, we must stop judging. Matthew 7:1 states, "Do not judge, or you too will be judged" (NIV). Jesus tells us how to get out of that ditch, by doing something within our power. *Decide to stop being critical of others.* While you're at it, stop criticizing *yourself!* After becoming aware of this issue, I began noticing how every critical thought about others manifested in my own life.

I judged a friend's kids for being careless with valuables, leaving leather coats at sporting events, their Bibles at church, and expensive sunglasses at our house. Then, I left my cell phone at that friend's house! Ouch!

Shocked by the volume of lost and found items at our local elementary school, I allowed negative thoughts to run through my mind about irresponsible parents and children. Then I found my water bottle among the items. Oops!

I love to go thrift store shopping and garage sale exploring. Occasionally, I find a brand- new item with the original store tag still on it! I think, *How wasteful! Why isn't that item returned to the store for a refund?*

Then, while in grad school, I needed a new dress for a special occasion, and I didn't have time to shop, so I grabbed the best one available at the only store I visited, thinking I would make do if I didn't have time to shop again before the party. Well, another opportunity to speed shop came up, and I found a gown I liked better. I determined to return my mediocre find as soon as I had another break in my schedule. By the time that happened, I couldn't find the receipt. By the time I found the receipt, it was past time to return the item. I became the person I judged, donating something with the tag on it. Whack!

That judgment took 30 years to come around, but it got me!

Each judgment that pops into our heads comes back to haunt us. Every time. If you don't believe me, start jotting down the negative thoughts you have towards others and then take inventory in your own life. Did you do that in the past, or is it currently happening in some way? If not, just wait. . . . it may take many years!

Before my eyes were opened, I prided myself on being non-judgmental. Apparently, I was deceiving myself. Once full awareness of the immutability of this law became evident, I saw the swift boomerang hit me every time I judged, or even thought of an individual in a critical way! It was horrifying to think of how many negative experiences I must have brought into my life, unaware of my part in causing them through my judgments. The connection was there; I was just blind to it before! That realization convinced me of the urgency to work on overcoming my negative, self-righteous ways.

DEFEND/DEFLECT

That brings us to the last of the ABCDs. When I defend or deflect, I simply turn the attacking, blaming, and critical accusations back on the person who is doing it to me. It's like I've got a shield up to turn all the arrows coming at me back to the attacker. The axiom "Sticks and stones may break my bones, but words will never hurt me" was often repeated during my childhood. In other words, I was taught to deny the pain of how I felt when someone said or did something hurtful. I discovered that most of the world has been conditioned to do that, too.

I did not have a framework to express my feelings in a healthy way, in a manner that the other person could hear or understand, and neither had I been taught how to listen to others in a way in which they felt heard. A critical piece of education was lacking, through no fault of my parents or the system.

On top of that, when I was sad, upset, or had other negative emotions, they were frequently denied ("You shouldn't feel that way"), minimized ("Someone else has it a lot worse than you"), discounted ("That's nothing; it's not a big deal"), shamed ("How dare you say that?"), labeled ("How stupid!"), blocked ("I don't want to hear that!"), punished ("Go to your room!"), or ignored. Rarely were they validated. The lesson to me was clear: *My feelings don't count*. It took a long time for me to realize that was a lie. They *do* count.

Frequently, I hear others comment, "They don't care how I feel." I remember feeling that way, too. Little did I know that I looked to others to care about my feelings. When they didn't, I subconsciously stopped caring about my own feelings as well.

POINTS TO PONDER:

- Attacking/Accusing involves telling someone what to do, what they did to us, labels their behavior, or includes a negative tone
- Blaming puts all the fault on someone else
- Criticizing focuses on the flaws of others
- Defending or deflecting puts the responsibility back on others or denies ownership
- These approaches leave us feeling frustrated and powerless
- We need to learn a new approach

Now that we've picked our way over some steppingstones, let's find the path to empowerment.

CHAPTER 11

PATH TO EMPOWERMENT:
HOW TO STOP ATTACKING AND ACCUSING

"Everyone thinks of changing the world,
but no one thinks of changing himself."
—Leo Tolstoy

My husband and I had made some progress, but becoming aware of the ABCDs opened the door to an entire new landscape of healing for us.

Knowing that attacking/accusing, blaming, criticizing, and defending/deflecting led to feelings of powerlessness, I began looking very intentionally for ways to replace powerlessness with empowerment.

This process began with looking for viable alternatives to attacking and accusing.

It's only when our relationship is at odds, there's tension between us, or the other person is mad at us for some reason, that our requests are met with resistance. In a crisis, such as when a kid is running full speed for the road into oncoming traffic, shouting,

"STOP!" is appropriate. There are certainly times we need to yell, "Don't!" even if we're not on the best of terms. Sticking fingers into electric sockets comes to mind. These are commands not requests.

I'd like to start a movement to change how we relate to others by validating their feelings, starting with the people in my life. Oh, and I must not forget to validate my own feelings! It has not been easy, nor without lots of ditch diving (meaning that I resort to my old ways, sometimes more than I remember to implement my new behaviors). Just as it takes a big ship considerable time to turn around, changing our ways of relating will take a long time, as well. But it's worth the effort!

Identifying my feelings about the matter turned out to be a key ingredient. After spending most of my life believing my feelings didn't matter, it surprised me to discover that I needed to figure out how I feel in order to crawl out of the ditch! At first, this was difficult. Taking inventory of my feelings was new to me. In fact, I struggled to figure out how I really felt! Sometimes I got in touch with one aspect of my emotions while ignoring other parts. I see this often in my practice. When people focus only on the good qualities of their significant other, they get married. When attention shifts to negative qualities, they get divorced. We need to consider both. At the same time. That's hard.

Before, I felt *powerless*, whether I recognized it or not, so how do I replace that with empowerment? I thought identifying one positive emotion to counter the negative would suffice.

If my child is not doing their homework, how do I feel about that? Beyond frustrated, that is. What lies beneath that concrete lid of powerlessness? A host of mixed feelings lie buried. No wonder I capped it off with cement! That's a lot easier and a whole lot less scary than digging up and identifying those hidden emotions.

Some of the feelings about my child's academics include: afraid their teacher won't know how smart they really are, that they'll flunk a grade, angry and frustrated because I don't know what I can do to get them to do the work, disrespected and disregarded by my kids for not listening to me, and feeling like a failure as a mom.

Taking stock of *all* the ways I feel provides valuable input on what course of action to take. This eventually evolved into a first step involving four parts. With all that information, I can now think of options that once escaped me.

If my spouse isn't bringing home flowers, how do I feel about it? Well, for me, I'd much rather he spends money on taking me out to dinner, doing something to improve the house, or going on a trip. However, other emotions might include feeling unappreciated, unloved, ignored, or not valued. Communicating how I feel and what I want is necessary. Maybe learning Gary Chapman's, *The Five Love Languages,* would help.

Because of my upbringing, I believed that if my husband loved me, he'd know what I wanted and how I felt. That is the biggest lie! Well, maybe there are bigger lies, but other people only know what we want if we express our desires clearly. Hinting, beating around the bush, assuming the other person knows, and other oblique approaches do a disservice to both my mate *and me.* However, as a child I learned these unhealthy tactics. Because I wasn't direct or forthright about what I wanted, I often didn't get my needs met. I had been conditioned to give up what I wanted, so I sacrificed many of my desires needlessly.

How do we ever really know what another person wants? *They tell us!* That's the best, most healthy way to be in relationship. Let other people know how you feel and what you want in a way that is not demanding but straightforward and clear.

The remedy for my ineffective way of relating started with identifying my feelings about the topic at hand. *All of them.* Was I mad, sad, angry, or glad? This took some practice and time. A variety of tools are available to help with this process. A feeling wheel provides words to describe our emotions. It's available for free at http://feelingswheel.com. The more time I invested in taking stock of my feelings, the more it paid off down the road.

In the past, I tended to make bipolar decisions either based solely on negative feelings or only considering positive aspects. Neither of those extremes got me where I wanted to go. They are ditches. Acknowledging both the negative *and* positive of any given topic is an "on the road" behavior, which we will discuss in detail.

The following steps helped me crawl out of my ditch littered with behaviors rendering me powerless. This is what I learned to do instead of attacking and accusing:

STEP 1: IDENTIFY HOW I FEEL

I begin by identifying all the ways I feel about the other person's action (or inaction).

And to do this, the first question I ask myself is: *"What is my motivation?"*

We always have a positive reason for why we want what we want, including both a personal and an altruistic motive for our desires. We want something for others and for ourselves too. Often, the self-protective drive is hidden from awareness. The outward stimulation may be: "I love you," "I want the best for you," "I want to protect you," or "I want to help." Inward or personal motivations have more to do with wanting to feel comfortable, safe, valued, accepted or wanting to protect yourself or your possessions.

A client suddenly broke off a relationship with a man she loved very much, citing the reason, "It was the wrong kind of relationship." Even though that part was true, much later she learned that the driving force behind this move was subliminal terror. She believed that he would eventually reject her. She cared about him so much that she didn't think she could survive rejection. However, this was hidden from her awareness.

Another example of others- and me-focused motivation relates to wanting my kids to do well in school. I knew good grades would provide the widest array of options in adulthood, and I desired that for them. I also wanted to look good as a mom (my hidden reason), especially since I was PTA president. My efforts to get them to do their assignments were limited to asking if they had homework, nagging, pleading, raising my voice, or threatening to take away privileges. None of those methods worked well. It never once occurred to me to tell them the reasons *why* I wanted them to do homework.

People get into fights motivated by a drive to protect self, possessions, or reputation. Even though their actions are negative, the individual is striving to protect. That points out the importance of discovering our overt and covert stimuli.

After identifying the altruistic and personal motivation, I ask myself a second question: *"What are my positive thoughts and feelings about the situation?"*

Positive thoughts and feelings I had about my kids and school included: They are smart, inquisitive, intelligent, attentive, and pick up ideas quickly. I love being around them, and most of the time they are well behaved. I know they can do well when they attend to a matter. They persevere when learning something that captures their interest.

Once all positive thoughts and feelings have been noted, I ask myself a third question: *"What are my negative thoughts and feelings about the situation?"*

My negative thoughts and feelings included frustration that my children often weren't self-motivated to do their homework. I was angry when they didn't turn in assignments and felt powerless to make them give priority to their schoolwork. As a kid, I was self-motivated to do homework and it never crossed my mind to *not* turn in an assignment. Therefore, I didn't understand why they weren't as motivated as I, nor did I know how to pass on that value to them. I was mad at myself for failing to teach them to value learning the same way I did.

Once the negatives have been expressed, I focus on the answer to a fourth question: *"What are my underlying fears?"*

Many fears hid beneath my negative thoughts and feelings, of which I was not consciously aware. I feared: my kids wouldn't be able to achieve their full potential; was concerned they would fail; feared they wouldn't learn what they needed to know; worried that they would end up with low self-esteem; anxious that I would look bad as a mom; and preoccupied with thinking I wasn't doing a good job as a parent.

This fourth question turned out to be super important. When fear remains undetected, it drives the bus. We tend to try to avoid what we fear by ignoring the problem and procrastinating, which contributes to pulling into our lives the very thing of which we're afraid. Often, sharing our fears diminishes or dispels them.

The more I practiced answering these four questions, the more my motivations, feelings, and fears became evident. Eventually, I didn't have to write them down; I could do it in my head. It surprised me that I had so many fears driving my actions! Noting both the positive and negative helped me to see the range of feelings I experienced. Until I started doing this, I tended to just look at the positive feelings I had and proceed based on those. At other times, key life decisions resulted from overwhelming negative feelings. When only looking at half of the picture, decisions ended up being lopsided. Other times, when I was driven by fear and didn't examine feelings and motivations, I made the worst decisions.

Once both positive and negative ways I feel including fears about the topic have been identified, I'm in the best position to figure out what I am going to do about how I feel. There can be lots of feelings that range from a host of fears all the way to the opposite end of the spectrum of positive feelings. Often, talking with the person or people involved and sharing all those mixed feelings may resolve the issue.

However, discovering the best course of action sometimes requires more steps.

To stay out of the ditch and firmly centered on the road, I need to consider the thoughts, feelings, concerns, and desires of the other person and me, *and* value them equally.

STEP 2: IDENTIFY HOW THE OTHER PERSON FEELS
   A. Identify both self-protective and altruistic motivations of the person
   B. Name positive thoughts and feelings this individual holds
   C. Name negative thoughts and feelings this individual holds
   D. Identify their fears

Of course, *asking* how others feel is the best way to find out. However, that isn't always possible. If you know the person well, you can come up with a fairly accurate assessment of motivation, positive and negative thoughts and feelings, and fears. It's important to look at it from their perspective and not what you think and feel based on your pain.

I realize I often ascribed negative intentions to others, whereas I knew my motives were positive. I have since adjusted my thinking to believe that the other person has positive motivations as well, even if their actions are ditchy. It's just hard for me to believe that when I'm feeling hurt. For example, if someone punches someone in a barroom brawl, the action is driven by desire to protect reputation, physical safety, or the safety of another. The motivation is positive, even though the action hurts someone else.

Once you've gathered information on yourself and the other person, now you have as complete of a picture as possible to make a decision:

STEP 3: LOOK AT BOTH SIDES TO DECIDE WHAT TO DO

Figure out what *you* will do based on the above information, while at the same time taking into consideration the best option for the other person.

Looking at the situation from both perspectives increases the chances it will be the best for both of you. Sometimes you may decide in favor of what you want over the other person's wishes; at other times you will choose to sacrifice your preference on behalf of the other. This conscious thought process takes us out of the ditch of obligation to a place of choice; and therefore, we won't end up feeling resentful.

Jesus provided a great example for us when He chose to go to the cross. He considered His motivation: He wanted to save us from destruction, *and* He wanted a relationship with humans because He created us. He didn't want to go through the pain and suffering. However, He considered all the options and decided the best course for all concerned meant He'd die on the cross. His choice ultimately brought joy for Him and us! "For the joy that was set before him he endured the cross, scorning its shame" (Heb. 12:2, NIV). When we consider both others and self in the decision-making process, we end up with a win-win solution.

STEP 4: TAKE ACTION

Often the problem resolves by expressing all the ways you feel, sharing your fears, and understanding the other person's perspective.

Here are some ideas of how to do that:

Ask or state your request in a different way.
1. Change the way the request is phrased. Instead of saying "You need to do your homework," or "You can't go out to play until your homework is done," try "You may play as soon as your homework is done." Note how the first sentence gives the other person the power. The second sentence is framed in a negative way. In the third sentence, you have power of influence; there's a reward for doing what you'd like done. It's not a bribe. It gives the person free will to decide to do their homework on their own; and it empowers the other to become self-motivated. If the homework doesn't get done, the privilege of playing goes away. Cline & Foster give some great suggestions in "Turn Your Words to Gold" available online at https://www.loveandlogic.com/documents/turn-your-word-into-gold-school.pdf

2. State clearly what you want. Begin your statement with phrases such as "I would like," "I prefer," "I would rather," or "I want." It challenged me to change how I started sentences. I was unaccustomed to stating point blank what I wanted. I used to say, "Would you like to. . .," "Do you want. . .," "Why don't we. . .," "How about doing. . .," and "What do you think about. . .?" These are common ways of approaching an idea. People are smart enough to figure out that you also want what you're proposing, but it is framed in a way that gives the person we ask all the power, leaving us powerless.

Let's look closer at the dynamics of that approach: If the person I ask doesn't want to do what I offer, I feel stuck. If they say no, I feel rejected, with no recourse. I'd often come back with reasons why I wanted to follow through with my idea. Then my husband reacted with, "Why do you always challenge my decisions?" I felt shut down. Without realizing it, I gave away my power by asking what the other person wanted without being clear about what I want.

However, if I state what I desire first ("I want to go to the park, would you like to go?"), the other person can still say no, but now I have freedom to go to the park by myself or ask someone else to join me. It amazed me how empowering it felt to be direct with what I wanted. Of course, it has taken a long time to change such an ingrained habit. The old way still slips out from time to time.

Remember that others-focused people tend to end up in romantic relationships with me-focused people and vice versa. So, as an OF person, I'll still try to accommodate what you want no matter how it's expressed. A me-focused person tends not to be so inclined, and to take things literally. A MF person doesn't go through the mental gymnastics that OFs do to read between the lines.

At other times, it's better to approach with a starter such as: "This needs to be done by (state the time); will you do that?"

Asking "will you" gives the individual freedom to say no, which then requires us to figure out what we will do if the answer is no. That can be scary. However, when I thought about it, I got told "no" more often when I approached a question obliquely. The challenge lies in figuring out an appropriate action if we receive a negative response, and we may need help from someone else to determine what to do.

My old, people-pleasing ways were driven by fear, and I felt rejected when my ideas were turned down or someone didn't want what I wanted. I had to remind myself that I also have the right to say no when I don't want to do something. Deep down, I want to be free to be myself. I set myself and those around me free when I give others the freedoms I also desire. I must advocate for my preferences instead of relinquishing them.

The old way doesn't allow for a "no" to happen without conflict, rebellion, or disappointment. I would tell people what they needed to do and expect them to do it. When the other person refused to do what I wanted, I became frustrated, angry, and resorted to manipulation, control, bribery, begging, coercion, force, or other tactics to get my way. It didn't feel good for me or for the other person to do it that way. I may have gotten what I wanted, but it was done grudgingly, underhandedly, or resentfully.

I can tell my sixteen-year-old that his room needs to be cleaned by 5 p.m. on Friday and let him know *what I will do* if he decides not to do it. I inform him, "If your room isn't clean by then, I will pick up the clothes and other things lying in disarray and put them in storage for a week." It's not a threat; it's a statement of fact. I don't have to get mad if he doesn't do what I ask, because I have a plan of what I'm going to do next, and my son knows his favorite things will be unavailable for a week.

"If you don't clean your room, I'm taking away the clothes that are laying around" comes across as a threat. However, "If your room isn't clean by 5 p.m., the clothes are going in storage for a week" is a calm statement proposing a consequence for inaction.

The clothes and toys only went to storage a few times for my teenager to decide he'd rather have access to his things. He then chose to clean his own room. It empowered him to be self-motivated; and I didn't have to be an angry, nagging mom. Unfortunately, I didn't learn that till my kids were almost grown; and I wasn't consistent with it, either. However, it's never too late to start, and whatever positive shifts we make change the trajectory for the better.

In Jonah 1:1–17 and 3:1–3, God asked Jonah to preach at Nineveh but didn't force him to go. Jonah said, "Thanks, but NO," and took off in the opposite direction. So, God took his boat away for three days. It was enough time for Jonah to decide to do what God asked.

It's critically important to be considerate of our children's belongings and not throw out or give them away. That would be hurtful. They would harbor bitter and angry feelings if that was done. It also reduces self-motivation. When deciding consequences, think about how you would feel if the consequence you are contemplating was levied on you.

Figuring out options for consequences presented a great challenge for me. I felt powerless because I had no clue what *I* could do differently. I needed help from others to brainstorm creative and effective ideas. You, too, might need assistance to come up with new approaches, and a professional coach or counselor can help.

When proposing to others places to go or things to do, offering two or three options instead of one increases the chance of finding mutual buy-in. My *old* way of suggesting an activity went like this: "Why don't we go hiking?" "Would you like to go out for Chinese food?" "Let's go to a movie." Only one option was offered. With that approach, we risk rejection or co-dependent compliance. Changing the phrasing to "I'd like to go for a hike, a walk, or a bike ride. What would you like?" or "Some restaurant options I'd like are Chinese, Italian, or French. Do any of those appeal to you?" This approach feeds my desire to please others while at the same time considering my own wishes. When I propose three options I am interested in pursuing, it increases the likelihood that we will agree on one. It's a win-win, and we are both happy. It also leaves the discussion open for the other person to add a suggestion. Offering choices side-steps someone feeling obligated because no other options were presented, or feeling rejected because someone said no to the one recommendation offered.

The shift in approach ensures freedom for me and allows the other person to also be free. When I can figure out what I will do if the other person doesn't choose to do what I want, we both feel empowered, increasing our willingness to cooperate instead of resist.

Respond Instead of Reacting

When someone yelled at me, said hurtful things, or became aggressive, I used to stay there and take it or react in kind. I've since learned to use my voice. . .in a different way. Instead of yelling back, now I either take a time out or a moment to identify how I'm feeling (which is hard in the middle of being triggered), and then I figure out what to do.

Often, it entails me leaving the room or the conversation. I used to storm out silently or slam the door on my way out; it may have communicated my anger, but it did nothing to motivate a shift in behavior. Now, I can respond with: "I refuse to tolerate that kind of treatment anymore." I explain what was said or done that hurt me. For example: "When you said that, I felt hurt."

I might say: "If you say that again, I'm going to leave for fifteen minutes, and then I will return." Each time it occurs, increase the length you're gone. "If you do that again, I'll leave for thirty minutes." If the person becomes aggressive, I might respond by saying something like, "I will leave for six hours." If you are in physical danger, call the cops. I'm not forcing the person to be different. I'm just not going to stick around for someone to insult me, if that is what they choose to do. Key elements of this approach include: letting the person know what you will do if they do something that hurts you; taking action where you can increase time increments or ratchet up consequences; stating when you will return; and assuring the other person that you will not abandon the relationship, just the behavior. We all need time to change reactions.

Without knowing it, I *allowed* others to hurt me because I didn't know how to protect myself in a healthy way. I'd bury my hurt instead of vocalizing it. If I exited, I didn't explain why. The other person was left to make up their own story about what was going on. Because of our tendency to blame the other person, the connection between their actions and my hurt got drowned in my silence. When I felt hurt by my spouse's actions, my abrupt withdrawal without explaining that I would return, triggered his fear of abandonment. That spurred him to act in rejecting ways. Of course, cluelessness blinded both of us. However, it's never too late to learn.

Seek wisdom and guidance from God

God can help us see things we miss and give inspiration for what to do about the issue. Read the Bible to gain understanding on an issue. Ask God where to go in the Bible and follow the inspiration you get.

STEP 5: LET GO OF THE OUTCOME

After taking all aspects into consideration, valuing self and others equally, we usually land on the best choice. After deciding upon a course of action, don't worry about how you think others will respond. I had to learn to tolerate my spouse's displeasure when I decided, from my perspective, the best option when it ran against his preference. Once I started doing that, to my surprise, he often came to accept my point of view.

Becoming empowered requires me to face my fear of a negative reaction. I've already thought about the issue from their perspective, and I have also considered what's best for me. If I worry about how they will react or what they will think, I'm falling back into manipulation, by *trying to get a desired response from the other by what I do.*

I spent my life trying to figure out how my spouse would react to any given situation; that's a part of what kept me powerless. I *guessed* at what he'd do, with just enough accuracy to conclude that he would react unfavorably even if I did things differently. So many times, I let my anticipation of the reaction I'd get paralyze me into inaction. That's a sure way to stay locked in powerlessness. I talked myself out of a lot of healthy moves because I feared the repercussions.

Men often think, "If I bring home flowers, I'll get lucky." Women may reason, "If I fix a nice dinner, he'll fix the leaky faucet." Both of those examples carry hidden expectations of getting something in exchange for the "thoughtful" action. The intent of getting something in response to giving something boomerangs. Most often, our partner does not pick up on the expectation, so it leaves the expectant person disappointed. Or if the nicety is thinly veiled, the partner sees the strings attached and feels resentful for the manipulative approach. The new way of responding does not include anything underhanded, contrived, or misleading to coerce the other into complying with your wishes.

Our actions must be free of obligations, either overt or covert. Making the shift from manipulation to influence feels great. We celebrate our own freedom when we grant others theirs.

It may be true that my spouse doesn't react to my action in the way I'd like, but I'm often surprised at the positive long-term effect. And when we no longer allow others to speak or act in degrading ways towards us, we are doing them a favor too, because we prevent them from acting in sinful ways towards us.

A client said, "I told my husband that I felt put down when he made a derogatory comment about my hair."

The first time it happened, he reacted in a dismissive way and replied, "I was just joking."

She followed the comment with, "Well, it still hurt my feelings."

The next time he made a hurtful comment to her, she said, "What you said hurt. I'm going to leave the room if you say that again." She reported that it only took two or three times for him to quit making those kinds of comments!

You won't know for sure if it will work or not until you try it. That's also why it's important to have a plan to ratchet up the consequences. Responding in a different way only once will not bring permanent change. It's the accumulation through repetition that makes a difference over time, and it may take fifty repitions.

Freedom comes when I make decisions independent of anticipated reactions. If I've thought about both my partner's needs and mine at the same time, it probably is the wisest choice. That doesn't mean he will necessarily like it.

The steps listed above address ways we can avoid attacking or accusing others. Instead of waiting on others, hoping they will make the move we want, we become empowered to act. We no longer feel frustrated, angry, and powerless when we can figure out what to do about a situation. I quickly understood the concept, but I'm still working on changing how I do life, even though I've been practicing this for several years!

Now that we have identified ways to shift from telling others what to do and figured out how to act on our own behalf, in the next chapter we'll examine how to shift away from our tendency to blame others without taking all the blame ourselves, and learn what to do about criticism.

POINTS TO PONDER

- Consider your motivations for why you want what you want
- Identify positive and negative thoughts and feelings about the issue
- Name the fears
- Repeat the four-step process for others involved
- Decide what action to take
- Express yourself directly and offer options
- Take action
- Do not allow predicted reactions to stymie you. Let go of the outcome.
- Create consequences that can be increased incrementally

CHAPTER 12

PATH TO EMPOWERMENT:
HOW TO STOP BLAMING, CRITICIZING, DEFENDING, AND DEFLECTING

"Yesterday I was clever, so I wanted to change the world.
Today I am wise, so I am changing myself."
—Rumi

*I*n the last chapter, we covered empowering ways to combat the widespread habit of attacking and accusing, the "A" of the ABCDs. Now, we will examine how to get away from blaming, criticizing, and defending/deflecting.

Let's start with steps we can take to help us stop playing the blame game.

BLAME

Start by identifying your part in the problem.

Believe it or not, there is freedom in admitting what you do wrong and taking responsibility for it. The beauty of this is multifaceted. In dealings with others, we always play a part, whether it is large or small (sometimes as minute as "I happened to be there.") So, when I admit to my part of the problem, it lightens the load. For both of us. Plus, it's true. I did say or do something wrong whether it was my fault or not. Owning what I do wrong involves learning to let go of shame and guilt, which requires forgiving myself for my mistakes and others for theirs.

Apologize and forgive yourself for your part. Admitting to others when I messed up was hard at first. I wasn't used to doing that. Shame threatened to engulf me. Apologizing was hard, too, because I had to swallow false pride. However, it became easier with practice. It helps restore peace in the relationship.

It's important to only apologize for my part and not the pieces that weren't mine. My confession is much more genuine when I do that. For instance, if I track snow in on someone's carpet, and say, "I'm sorry it's snowing; I got snow on your carpet," I'm subtly putting the blame on the fact that it's snowing (which I did not make happen) and detracting from my part. In that example, I didn't even actually apologize for tracking in snow; I just announced that I did. I appreciate when others admit and apologize for their errors. Therefore, I'm practicing apologies such as, "I'm sorry I got your carpet wet."

Forgive yourself! We set ourselves free when we do that. Free from what? Free from the tendency to repeat the mistake. When I forgive myself for my errors, I allow for the Holy Spirit to move inside me to change. That also loosens the grip of shame and guilt. Jesus died on the cross for our sins, shame, and guilt. I could let go of the sins, but it was much harder to part with the shame and guilt. That may be a process.

Forgive the other person for their part. I already talked about how we set ourselves free when we forgive ourselves; therefore, you'd think that we set the other person free when we forgive them. But that's not true. We set ourselves free in this aspect as well! Until I forgive the other person for their part, I drag around negative thoughts, resentment, and bitterness toward that individual, like a cannon ball chained to my ankle. Forgiveness unlocks that shackle.

Does that mean the individual who hurt me runs free? Nope! God says, "Vengeance is mine; I will repay, saith the Lord" (Rom. 12:19, KJV). We need to trust that He has ways of doing that, even if we don't ever see how God evens the score. Truly, we don't get away with anything! I know *I* suffer for the hurts I cause others but believed the lie that if I forgive others for the ways they hurt me, the forgiven would walk away scot-free. People who hurt us do end up suffering, even if we cannot ascertain in what way. God is just.

Figuratively speaking, I placed people against whom I harbored resentments, bitterness, and unforgiveness in a storeroom in my mind. When someone hurt me, I hung them up in that room by the back of their collar, on a coat hook, with their feet dangling off the ground a few inches. Mentally, I locked them away, afraid they'd run free if I forgave, so I just kept them there. Then God taught me about forgiveness. When I finally forgave, it was as if I took those people off my hooks and transferred them to God's hooks for Him to handle.

Forgiving is freeing. . .for me. It also builds a bridge halfway towards the repair of the relationship. The person who hurt me has ownership of the other half of the bridge. Sometimes, if someone has injured us in serious ways, we forgive but hold a healthy boundary of not allowing that person back into our lives.

Brainstorm to find a solution. In the long run, it doesn't really matter whose fault it is. Though based on the lengths our society goes through to assure someone gets blamed, you'd never believe that. If we spent as much time discussing the problem and brainstorming to find a solution as we do on blame placement, a lot of lawyers would be looking for a new career.

While we're looking for someone to blame, the problem continues unaddressed. It is not as important *who* spilled the milk as who is going to clean it up. Focusing energy where it counts makes more sense.

What went wrong? How can we fix it? How can we prevent a recurrence in the future? **Those** questions provide productive answers, not *Whose fault is it?* Now that we know how to shift from a stance of fault finding by owning our part, forgiving self and others, and brainstorming to resolve the issue, let's learn how to cut out criticism.

CRITICISM

How do we stop criticizing each other? Three practices can be lifechanging:

Focus on the good, positive, and praiseworthy. The antidote to negatively judging others lies in shifting our focus from looking for flaws, faults, and failures to looking for the good, positive, and praiseworthy actions in others. Philippians 4:8 tells us to attend to things that are true, honest, just, pure, lovely, and of good report (KJV). Go one step beyond thinking about it. Act on this!

Cultivate a habit of complimenting others. Intentional, sincere compliments reduce negative behaviors, improve how others feel about themselves, and increase our own positive internal feelings all at the same time! I feel good when I genuinely praise someone for something, anything!

Over twenty years ago, while visiting Manhattan, I passed a woman walking in the opposite direction. She had gorgeous, long, flowing black tresses. Ignoring norms that caution against talking to strangers in New York City, I boldly blurted, "I love your hair!"

Surprised, she turned to see who had complimented her. "Thank you!" she exclaimed with a big smile.

Two people felt great in that moment. And I *still remember that brief encounter from over two decades ago!* Though the effects of most compliments fade long before that one did, the fact remains: the good things we say to others positively affect us.

A compliment makes two people feel better; a criticism makes two people feel worse. George Adams says, "We should seize every opportunity to give encouragement. Encouragement is oxygen to the soul."[1] How many of us grew up deprived of oxygen in our souls?

When the oxygen level drops on an airplane, we put our own mask on first. Be the first one to give out compliments and encouragement. That will restore the air supply in our families.

Shifting from a critical stance starts with deciding to begin commending others. Our world would be a better place if we all did this. If this is the only takeaway you get from this book, it will be well worth your time for reading this!

Before transitioning to the next point, one word of caution: Let go of all expectations of how you think the other person will respond. Compliments must have no strings attached. If you secretly think, *If I compliment him for this, then he'll praise me for something,* it will backfire. You'll be disappointed because you're not getting the response you hoped for.

A client tried complimenting others for a while. When I asked how it went, the response was: "I quit because I didn't get any compliments back." The expectation of a reciprocal reply negated the power of this way of living. Disappointment at not receiving praise in return also robbed that person of the joy of giving the accolades.

Even if no one ever compliments you for the rest of your life, keep the praises going! At least you'll feel good, and that improves how others experience you.

Be mindful about being grateful. Because I wasn't taught to be thankful as a child, creating a gratitude journal where I wrote five things I appreciated every day helped me shift from having a critical spirit to having a grateful spirit.

When I started keeping a gratitude journal, I was so used to focusing on the negative that it was difficult coming up with things I appreciated! I started by listing things about my family, my health, the weather, and comforts I enjoy. Since the only thing I'm consistent about is inconsistency, I did not write in my gratitude journal every day, but it was enough to get me to the place where I actually *felt* grateful.

Then when praying, instead of beginning my prayers with "please help," I switched to thanksgiving. "Thank you, God, for my family, for such a beautiful day, for sunshine, for the many blessings you have given me." The more I practiced thanksgiving, the richer I felt without any increase in pay. I was complimenting God on all the great things He did for me. God wants to know that I noticed, and I feel good because I'm telling Him that I recognize His providence.

Therefore, the antidote for criticism is focusing on the positive, complementing others, and being intentionally grateful. At first, I was afraid that if I stopped criticizing those around me, problems might get swept under the rug, but that's not the case. In fact, I soon discovered that my words of praise actually fostered better behavior in others! This is because, as humans, we crave positive affirmation. We also function better and solve problems better in a positive atmosphere.

Critical thoughts, disguised as discernment, became easier to challenge as time progressed. When something negative happens, I tell myself, "I could see myself doing that," or "I've done something like that before." This keeps my inner critic at bay. For example, when someone cuts in front of me in traffic, I think of times I've done that. The result? I feel compassion instead of anger.

Switching from criticism to compliments and focusing on the positive changed my outlook on life significantly!

That leads us to the final letter, D. Perhaps you already know what to do instead of defending or deflecting. Let's see if our remedies match up.

DEFEND/DEFLECT

This one is easy. When others become defensive with me, it usually means I'm attacking, accusing, blaming, or being critical. That reminds me to stop what I'm doing and *employ a different tactic*.

The key to changing this pattern lies in applying the alternatives to the ABCs of attacking, blaming, and criticizing that have been covered in this chapter.

I'm also learning to ask family members how they would like me to phrase requests in a way that's not so irritating to them.

MOVING FROM A, B, C, D TO E

When we stop attacking/accusing, blaming, criticizing, defending/deflecting, we really are free to move to E, which is empowerment. No longer is our wellbeing at the mercy of waiting for something from someone else. We are freer than ever to climb out of our ditches and stay balanced and moving forward.

POINTS TO PONDER:

- To halt blaming, identify your part, ask for forgiveness, forgive the other for their part, and brainstorm for a solution
- To Eliminate criticism, focus on the positive and praiseworthy, practice complimenting others, and develop an attitude of gratitude
- To end defending and deflecting, apply the alternatives offered instead of attacking, criticizing and blaming

CHAPTER 13

FROM THE OTHERS-FOCUSED DITCH TO THE ROAD

*"When you've spent your whole life listening to others,
it takes courage to pay attention to the sound of
your own voice."*
—Healthyplace.com

Once we grasp that fear and powerlessness have been driving our ditch behaviors, it's time to wrest the keys away from fear and put God behind the steering wheel. When we stop subconsciously following our fears and begin consciously following the prompting of the Holy Spirit, we find new freedom on the road.

After recognizing the behaviors to which I defaulted in the ditch, the next step was figuring out how to replace those ditchy doings with healthy patterns to keep me traveling forward.

Through this process, I've become a great fan of do-overs. Golfers call them mulligans. Make agreements with everyone around you to do real-time rehearsals. When the old, automatic reactions slip out and you or your partner recognize the old ditchy behaviors, immediate stop what you're doing and call for a do-over. Start the conversation over. Practice how you'd like to react instead. Include the other person in the process to come up with a way of phrasing that you both approve. We increase our skills more rapidly in a cooperative, rather than critical, environment.

Let's start with OF ditchy behaviors and identify some life-giving alternatives we can practice.

1. PEOPLE PLEASING

You can take the people pleaser out of the ditch, but they will always enjoy doing things for others, and that's a good thing. However, we want to replace ditchy motivations with truer, healthier incentives.

I know for me, what changed was the ongoing internal dialogue with myself. I don't always have to give up what I want to make others happy, though I will tend to lean in that direction more often than insisting on my own preferences. But more than ever before, I realize now that the goal is mutual happiness. My unhappiness negatively affects my spouse, and vice versa. We owe it to one another to be responsible for our own joy, thereby increasing mutual wellbeing.

Recently my husband and I were traveling on the last leg of our two-day return flight from Thailand. My husband's assigned seat was at the window and mine was on the aisle, with a stranger in the middle. The stranger offered to trade seats with me, in which case I would be the one stuck in the middle. In a way his offer to me instead of my husband made sense, as my husband's shoulders are broad, and he would have been quite squished in that middle seat.

The old me, without thinking, would have felt like I had no choice but to please everyone. I would have automatically taken the middle seat—yet felt resentful about it. The entire flight, I would have entertained negative thoughts about how selfish my spouse was for not offering to take the center seat. I'd have thrown a private pity party right there on the plane, squeezed in the middle seat, with no one else aware of my internal misery.

Instead, because I've been working on equally valuing my desires, I started by giving myself permission to politely decline the stranger's offer if I so chose. Now that I knew I could say yes or no, I got to decide—without resentment—what I wanted to do. Doing something kind for others became an option, not a compulsion I had to follow in order to win favor.

I decided I wanted to sit next to my husband while leaving him in the window seat where his broad shoulders would have more room. I changed seats, free from obligation and resentment, because I went through the thought process and determined the best option for all involved.

Perhaps on a future flight, under different circumstances, I might make a different choice. I evaluate circumstances on a case-by-case basis now, and what I want gets equal consideration. I know I will always lean toward putting myself second, and that's not a bad thing—Jesus put other's needs above His own, too. The difference is that He was never motivated by obligation or compulsion. He didn't serve others in a desperate hope to win their approval. He never carried resentment. The good He did emanated from a place of choice.

That's now my goal!

2. DEFAULT ANSWER "YES"

Two alternatives to this ditchy default are 1) giving myself time to think before answering, and 2) allowing myself to change my answer if I say yes too quickly.

To apply these options, I'm learning to say, "Let me think about that and get back to you." I know now that I need this time to identify what I want, consider all the perspectives, and pray before answering.

And because "yes" tends to ride on the tip of my tongue and sneak out before my brain engages, I'm learning how to give myself permission to change my mind. I'm giving myself latitude to say the words, "I said yes, but I didn't think it through. I want to ponder that some more and discuss the big picture with you." Another option? Saying "Oops, I reacted without thinking. I want to rethink whether I can truly say yes to that."

3. READILY GIVING UP WHAT I WANT

In the past, every time I defaulted to this ditchy behavior, I felt controlled without realizing I had *allowed* it.

As a child who had been given few choices in life, I subconsciously carried the lie into adulthood that what I wanted didn't matter. To be set free, this needed to stop.

I still tend to be quick to give up my preference when I'm on the fence about something, and changing this has been difficult. It takes concerted effort for me to advocate for myself. Sometimes, it's easier to go with the flow than slog through the process of figuring out if I truly want something or not.

But just because it's hard doesn't mean it's not worth it. As I continue working on this, being decisive about many things is easier than ever before. I'm able to express what I want most of the time; and if it's something I really want, I rarely hesitate to pursue it on my own. Before, if my husband wasn't interested in the same activity, fear of venturing out alone often kept me from doing it. I no longer forfeit fun things I like when he's not interested, nor do I try to talk him into joining me just because

I'm afraid to do things on my own. It's been freeing for both of us, and we're both a lot happier.

For example, I wanted to go on a hike and tour of Doi Inthanon while in Thailand recently. He wanted to explore coffee shops. I joined a tour group, and he met up with a fellow coffee aficionado. At the end of the day, we enjoyed reuniting and sharing stories of our experiences. He showed me pictures of the coffee shops he savored, and I got to show him pictures of the scenery the tour guide pointed out along the trail.

We both had a great day!

4. DIFFICULTY MAKING DECISIONS

For years, fear of making the wrong choice kept me paralyzed and in the land of indecision. A deeply rooted aversion to being blamed or criticized for choosing the wrong option drove me to give up my power and transfer responsibility for my preferences to others.

What are the alternatives I choose now? For starters, addressing that fear by deciding for myself and accepting responsibility for my mistakes has brought me much freedom and empowerment. It turns out that I like the decisions I make on my own behalf much better than those made by others for me, even when the option I choose isn't the best one.

Learning how to brainstorm options and evaluate pros and cons has brought me freedom from waffling and keep me traveling forward!

5. WALKING ON EGGSHELLS

Fear of the reactions of others underlies this behavior. What alternatives do we have?

Choices include being brave enough to put a name to our fears, brainstorming options, and deciding not to let fear keep us locked in the silent chamber.

When I learned how to muster the courage to say what needs to be said—and stopped believing it was my job to smooth any feathers that got ruffled as a result—I reached a turning point in my journey out of the OF ditch.

6. DIFFICULTY EXPRESSING FEELINGS OR OPINIONS

My conclusion as a child was that if no one else cared about my feelings or opinions, then neither did I. That doesn't make sense on paper, but it's a common reaction when children feel neglected or invalidated. (I wonder how many generations that goes back?)

What's the replacement?

It starts with consciously choosing to value my own feelings and opinions. And *that* started with the hard step of identifying my feelings and opinions—and then sharing them out loud. A Celebrate Recovery group helped immensely with this process because I learned that I was not alone in my struggle, and I felt accepted unconditionally in this group. Plus, I got to practice talking about my feelings in three- to five-minute segments.

Taking these little steps to become vulnerable with people I didn't know was like going to an emotional gym. Over time, I gained strength to start sharing my feelings and opinions at home.

Another key was learning to name the emotions I experienced. Often, they bounced around inside me, a mixture of positive and negative feelings and fears. Identifying and putting words to them freed them from the ditch where I kept them buried.

7. AVOIDING

I used to avoid topics and issues that caused conflict. I side-stepped arguments, sweeping things under the rug, hoping that time would dissipate the problem, and often it did.

What approaches have I learned to embrace?

Relationship Enhancement's (RE) ten skills provided me with tools to address conflict and discuss difficult topics within a framework of safety. RE taught me how to listen in a way that others felt heard, express myself more effectively, talk through conflict, and find win-win solutions to topics that used to be "hot buttons" for us. Descriptions of these ten tools are available through Nire.org.[1] There you can also access the International Directory of RE Providers or go online to CoupleTalk.com.[2]

My husband and I both began to learn and apply these tools. As we were learning, our old behaviors reared their ugly heads more often than not. However, as we have continued practicing this new way of communicating, our ability to work through emotionally charged issues has improved radically and continues to grow.

8. CO-DEPENDENCE

In the past, to feel okay about myself, I needed others to like me. Facing my fear of rejection did wonders to help me climb out of that pit. God loves me and will always be with me even if others reject me. That set me free from the slavery of worrying about what people think and whether others accept me. I don't like everyone on the planet; therefore, if some people don't like me, I will survive. Letting go of the need for everyone to like what I like or agree with me frees me from my addiction to approval from others. I don't need to prove *anything* to God, thankfully!

Letting go of co-dependence involved figuring out how to be in control of myself, stop allowing others to control me, and stop attempting to control others by telling them what they should or shouldn't do. Counselors and recovery groups helped a lot with this process.

9. BLAMING

We've covered alternatives to blaming in the last chapter but let me add this here.

Freedom from blaming others started first with swallowing my self-righteous pride, and then identifying and acknowledging my part. This is particularly hard when the other person carries the lion's share of fault. While it is completely true that others have done horrendous things and may be responsible for huge problems in my life, blaming disempowers me. I've lost enough; I don't want to give them any more ground. When I blame, I'm announcing to myself and to the world that I'm a victim. Even if I was, I don't want to do that anymore.

It's important to *only* express remorse for your role. Apologizing for more than that takes away from the sincerity of it, and it's not true. I used to take blame for things that weren't solely on me, but that doesn't serve me or anyone else.

Sometimes my part in the issue is simply, "I was there." Sometimes it's: "That was the family into which I was born." "I couldn't speak up," "I was threatened into silence," "I participated," or "I was too terrified or ashamed to say anything." That could be true for many reasons, especially when victimized as a child. Whether we chose our actions or were forced to do something against our will, we carry shame and guilt for what happened. Whatever role you played, whether passive or active, acknowledging your part is the first step in shifting from blame to empowerment. As weird as this sounds, we need to forgive ourselves for being there and God for allowing it to happen. Owning my share when mistakes are small helps build internal strength to take responsibility when I make big mistakes.

The second step was apologizing for the piece that's mine and asking forgiveness. If you suffered from childhood abuse, maybe the only apology is to God for the lies you believed about Him and about yourself because of what happened.

Third, I had to forgive the other person for their part. The bigger the offense, the harder it is to forgive. Asking God to give me the power to forgive clears out the darkness inside. Often, we need help through prayer, a therapist, or a recovery group to accomplish this task. The process for me began with: "God, every cell in my body wants to hold onto unforgiveness. The pile You're asking me to forgive feels bigger than Mt. Everest. I don't want to forgive, but that's Your desire for me. Give me the power to forgive what I cannot do on my own." That prayer cracked my walled-up heart and allowed the light and love of God to drive in a wedge and expand it, much like water widening a fissure in a rock. Over time, forgiveness became possible, and I finally became free!

Jesus died for our sins, guilt, and shame. Often, we accept the sacrifice for sin but hold on to guilt and shame. We need to let those go as well.

I used to think that forgiveness set the *other* person free. It doesn't. If they want freedom, they must do their own work. My forgiveness work accomplishes my own freedom from resentment, obsession, anger, rage, and revenge (which only backfires). I also sleep better, my stomach feels better, and my physical health improves (my joint pain went away after I forgave!). I also have more brain space to think of positive things. Furthermore, choosing to forgive myself for what I've done releases me from repeating mistakes.

The final step in gaining freedom from blame is brainstorming for a solution to how to move forward, fix the problem, or patch up the relationship if appropriate.

10. BEING PASSIVE

Stepping out of passivity requires me to first figure out what I want. Habitually giving up my desires rendered that muscle atrophied and weak, and it took time to exercise. At first it didn't feel like it was worth the effort; it felt so hard! Advocating for my desires started with identifying the things I really did care about. It was rocky and not pretty, but I steadily gained ground by standing up for my wishes. When it's a healthy desire, it benefits both of us, even when the other person initially opposes the idea.

For example, on our last trip to Thailand, I wanted to go to Chiang Rai, mostly to visit the foundation our friends supported and to visit the famous Buddhist White Temple. My husband had no interest in those two things, but because I was determined to go, he chose to go with me. He wanted to see a coffee plantation, but there had been no opportunity for that this trip. Little did we know, the organization we visited had a direct connection to a coffee business, and we got an unexpected visit and tour of both a coffee plantation and operation. We both ended up getting to do what we wanted! Pursuing my desire blessed us both!

11. FEELING OBLIGATED

Climbing out of the ditch of obligation onto the road of responding from choice involved consciously evaluating situations that triggered my "I have to" belief.

I started asking myself: Is this truly something that only *I* can do? What are the pros and cons of me fulfilling that "obligation"?

Is there something more important that I need to do? Can I delegate the task?

There are things I still don't want to do but choose to do anyway because it's the best for all involved, including me.

Jesus' decision to go to the cross to pay for our sins provides an excellent example of how He took it from an obligation to a choice. He did not want to go through the suffering, and even prayed these words: "Father, if you will, please don't make me suffer by having me drink from this cup. But do what you want, and not what I want" (Luke 22:42, CEV).

But He took the time to consider the needs of everyone involved. Jesus wanted a relationship with us, and we couldn't bridge the gap or clear out our sins ourselves. Therefore, He made the powerful choice to lay down his life: "No one takes my life from me. I give it up willingly! I have the power to give it up and the power to receive it back again, just as my Father commanded me to do" (John 10:18, CEV).

Before, I did not believe I had a choice; but now that I know I do, it's my responsibility to practice choosing wisely.

12. BEING RESENTFUL

When acting out of obligation, resentment tags along, which leaks out in hurtful ways towards others. It's better not to do something than do it out of obligation.

Forgiving people for the ways I felt obligated also releases resentment.

13. BEING SARCASTIC

I don't like it when others are sarcastic with me, so I need to be the change I want to see happen in my life. Instead of making thinly veiled sideways comments, what is a better approach?

For starters, I need to stop and consider what I really want or need to say. I may require time to sort through how I think and feel about the situation and consider how to frame my concern in an uplifting way, and then meet with the individual privately instead of commenting in front of others. Refer to Chapters 9 and 11 regarding choice of words and identifying your own feelings.

It's so easy to say things in our automatic ditchy ways; it takes conscious effort to choose heathier, life-giving forms of communication! It's difficult to change our old patterns but not impossible. Even poorly executed attempts provide steppingstones towards improvement.

14. BEING CRITICAL AND/OR GOSSIPY

When I speak in a disparaging way about someone to a third party, I'm gossiping or being critical.

What can be done instead?

Commit to looking for things worthy of praise and appreciation. Because of my lifelong habit of viewing others in negative ways, I am challenged to look only for good and speak positive words. I feel so much better about myself when I do! If I have an issue with my husband, I now talk to him directly about it instead of going behind his back to complain. I lived unaware of how my disparaging thoughts and comments affected both of us negatively. Criticizing others turns out to be lose-lose.

I don't want people gossiping about me. I have no power over what they do, but I do have power over what I do. I feel better internally when I lift others up. Imagine how much better our world would be if we each took it upon ourselves to only build up with our words instead of tear down! When I speak genuinely kind words, I feel good for saying it, and the other person feels good for receiving positive comments. That's a win-win.

That even lines up with Paul's exhortation: "Finally, my friends, keep your minds on whatever is true, pure, right, holy, friendly, and proper. Don't ever stop thinking about what is truly worthwhile and worthy of praise" (Phil. 4:8, CEV). I learned the opposite growing up; now I'm much happier because I'm dwelling on the positive.

We were in Thailand recently with a World Race group, and I was enjoying a cool drink in the afternoon heat with parents and their racers. The discussion turned to the power of words. World Racer Abigail Jernigan shared something she had learned that bears repeating: "Words are powerful! Therefore, they should only be used to bless, heal, and prosper."

I love that!

15. STUFFING MY HURTS

When I used to feel hurt, I held it in and didn't talk about it. Now, I discuss my feelings directly with the person who offended me. It took a long time to get there, but it's been worth the effort. Identifying my feelings, understanding what caused the hurt, and bringing it up to the other person in a way that does not attack, accuse, or blame helped me to succeed in this area. For more information on how to do this, CoupleTalk or Relationship Enhancement can help.

16. BEING PASSIVE-AGGRESSIVE

I hate it when others act in passive-aggressive ways, but I did the same thing most of my life!

What are other options? You may already know the remedy to this, because healthy on-the-road behaviors involve directness, honesty about feelings, and valuing self equally with others. Instead of acting in oblique, revengeful ways, we can resolve the issue by calmly and sincerely discussing what happened to cause upset and what to do to change it.

17. WITHDRAWING

While withdrawing from a situation may be the healthiest thing to do from time to time, *how* it's done determines whether it's a road or ditch behavior. If I'm leaving out of fear and don't explain why, I'm in the ditch.

What's the alternative? Communication. I need to let the other person know the reason I'm upset and how I won't tolerate being treated. I can say something like, "It hurts me when you say that, and I'd like you to apologize." If insulting comments are made again, consider a consequence with which you are willing to follow through.

Speaking up about and removing your presence from someone who hurt you for a defined amount of time may not seem very effective, but the results over time may surprise you. Because the greatest fear for a MF person is abandonment, leaving their presence is a form of abandonment, but commitment to return inspires the individual to reconsider their actions. Remember, we all switch ditches; therefore, we also shift between fear of abandonment and fear of rejection. Your decision not to put up with bad behavior by leaving the presence of the person for a defined period gives them time to think about improving their actions on their own.

This approach also empowers me without controlling the other person. I'm not telling them *not* to do what I don't like; I'm just not going to stick around if that's what the other person chooses to do.

Withdrawing from physically aggressive people works the same way. When we communicate why we are leaving, the conditions necessary upon return, and when we will come back, we increase our influence. Physically aggressive people are stuck deep in fear, and withdrawal triggers the terror of past experiences of abandonment. If they continue being physically aggressive, a permanent exit may become necessary.

18. SHUTTING DOWN

Shutting down occurred when I didn't know what to say and felt utterly trapped.

What can be done instead? Requesting a time-out so I can have time to gather my thoughts and process all the feelings bombarding me helps get me on the road. Journaling is also beneficial. What *is* the fear? What caused the paralysis? What do I want to say or have happen? I may need a couple of hours to sort it out. Then I must commit to discuss the situation after I've thought it through instead of reverting to my old tendency to sweep it under the rug.

19. EXPERIENCING CHAOS

Trying to make everyone happy is like spinning multiple plates. Eventually there are too many to keep going, and they start to fall and break. That's when life gets chaotic.

This has been a life-long struggle for me.

What's the alternative?

Taking time to list things I want to accomplish, prioritizing my obligations, figuring out what to let go, and learning to say no are empowering choices that reduce the chaos.

As I write these words, I realize I need to pare down even more because I do not have enough of a margin to chill, exercise, or spend as much time with my family as I'd like.

Ah, the process continues!

20. PLAYING THE VICTIM

This is more of an attitude I have or lie I tell myself based on the truth of having been victimized in some way in my past. The feeling of powerlessness pervades my life as long as I believe I'm stuck and must wait on others for change to happen.

An empowering alternative involves choosing to figure out what I can do about my situation, and then acting on that solution. Refer to Chapter 16 for ways to address the fears that attach to powerlessness.

21. WANTING TO SELF-HARM

When I turn to self-harm, whether it be overeating or attempting suicide, I'm feeling so powerless that I don't know what else to do. I sink to extreme fear based on a belief that I have no other options. Of course; that's a lie, but when in that place, it feels true.

Alternatives include seeking help. Naming all my fears also helps me climb out of this ravine. Keep naming your fears until they're all down on paper. Then look at Chapter 16 for ideas to combat these lies.

Now that we've examined alternatives to OF ditchy behaviors, let's take a look at alternatives to MF behaviors.

POINTS TO PONDER:
- Consider typical go-to ditch behaviors
- Identify fears driving those behaviors
- What alternatives can be employed instead?

CHAPTER 14

FROM THE ME-FOCUSED DITCH TO THE ROAD

"You can't stop being afraid just by pretending everything that scares you isn't there."
—Michael Mars

As we become more aware, our abilities to ditch our subconscious reactions for intentional responses grows, too. As we heal, these mindful choices begin to feel more natural than we ever thought possible.

Here are some alternatives to MF ditchy reactions. They may feel awkward and unfamiliar in the beginning, but practiced with intention, these life-giving alternatives transform our lives and our relationships.

1. BEING SELFISH

We all have a selfish streak. Becoming conscious of that is our first step out of the ditch. The truth is that attending to my desires without regard to how it affected others did *not* make me happy;

in fact, it left me feeling empty. However, my selfish behaviors continued as long as I remained blinded to the effect they had.

So, what other options exist?

On the road, caring for others *and* having what I want is possible. There, I can enjoy my possessions and experience contentment knowing I help to provide for others' needs as well.

The antidote to selfishness is giving. God provides a template for giving, plus He promises a great reward for stepping out in faith. "Begin by being honest. Do honest people rob God? But you rob me day after day. You ask, 'How have we robbed you?' The tithe and the offering—that's how! And now you're under a curse—the whole lot of you—because you're robbing me. Bring your full tithe to the Temple treasury so there will be ample provisions in my Temple. *Test me in this* and see if I don't open up heaven itself to you and pour out blessings beyond your wildest dreams. For my part, I will defend you against marauders, protect your wheat fields and vegetable gardens against plunderers" (Malachi 3:8–11, MSG, emphasis mine).

God not only promises ample provisions; He provides protection way beyond what any security system or identity theft insurance can offer. If everyone gave a tenth of their increase to the charities or churches that God puts on their hearts to support, every need would be met.

When my husband and I began tithing, stepping out in faith felt scary, and it seemed like we were just barely getting by. But over time God steadily provided. We kept track of His interventions, including the protection and safety we have enjoyed, and I'm blown away by the ways God has blessed us.

Over the years, God steadily granted us increase, and now we're getting to live our dream of traveling a lot. I'm amazed at how God brought it about! He truly has blessed us beyond my wildest dreams. We consistently see God's blessing for our commitment to being generous with donations.

2. DEFAULTING TO "NO"

"No" falls out of the mouths of MF people as fast as "Yes" does for OFs.

What can we do instead?

The same principle applies for both. Both sides need time to think about the topic before giving an answer. "Let me think about that and get back to you" buys time to consider all the aspects and pray about it before deciding.

Second, backtracking works just as well for coming out of this ditch. "I said no, but I want to consider it more. Let's discuss it after I've had time to do some research." Another way to say it could be: "I'm working on looking at all the angles before I answer. I'll talk about it after I've looked into it." Then set a time to revisit the subject.

3. BEING A PERFECTIONIST

There's a fine line between excellence and perfectionism. Excellence allows us to enjoy our creations, whether it's a delicious meal, an engaging painting, an exquisite musical score, a clean house, or our daily job. All of us appreciate excellence and applaud the efforts of others when it is achieved. When we strive for excellence and attain it, we feel deep satisfaction.

Perfectionism, however, steals our joy because fear whispers, "It's not good enough." No matter how impeccable the creation, the creator sees the flaws. Caught on a gerbil wheel of needing to be 100 percent leaves no room for peace or enjoyment of your accomplishment.

What's the alternative? Combating the fear of imperfection requires eradicating the lie that you must be perfect to be loved, overcoming the fear of not being good enough, and dispelling the misbelief that it's possible to be perfect.

Some ways to address it include praying about it, doing Emotional Freedom Technique, or going to counseling. The goal is to hold on to excellence while letting go of the stress of trying to attain perfection.

4. NEEDING TO BE RIGHT

Often, the MF *is* right, which leads to pride for that person and dependency for their mate. Topics we have strong convictions about, such as religion and politics, tend to be ones we have an "I'm right" attitude about.

Convinced the religion I espoused was "right" and all others were wrong, I believed for many years that mine was "the true church" and every other church was false. Eventually, God revealed that the organization I believed wholeheartedly to be the truth, the whole truth, and nothing but the truth was wrong on several key points. That caused the church to disintegrate, rocked my world, and taught me to hold loosely to what I believe, *even when convinced I'm right.* That experience proved to me that I can be certain I'm right, but still be wrong!

We can either insist on being right *or* have a relationship. Often, it's not possible to have both. The truth is that people who disagree with me when I'm staunchly holding to my position often withdraw, leaving me alone with my convictions.

Developing a humble attitude and recognizing that there is always a chance that I'm wrong has helped me to let go of my tendency to insist on being right. Now I hold most tightly to "we see through a glass darkly" (1 Corinthians 13:12, KJV).

5. HAVING DIFFICULTY SEEING OTHER PERSPECTIVES

In my me-focused ditch I can only see my own perspective. I'm so fixated on it that I can't pull away far enough to imagine how others may see things differently. It's especially hard when it's something I feel strongly about or want very much. When I'm in conflict with another, I don't *want* to see their perspective.

How do we combat our tunnel vision? Recognizing this tendency helps me become conscious of the need to look at the situation from other viewpoints, invite others to share their perspectives, and listen to understand. Acknowledging that I struggle to see an issue the same way someone else does paves the way for others to admit that they may also have a hard time seeing things the way I do. Thinking back, many times I believed my stance to be correct, only to discover later that I was wrong.

Perspective is like looking at the four walls of a room. In my sunroom, the west wall is solid windows to the peak of the cathedral ceiling, and it looks out onto a collection of trees. When I only look through those windows, I feel like I'm in a forest. The north windows reveal I'm in a housing development as I gaze over several roofs. The south view opens to our backyard, where I see kids jumping on the trampoline. There are no windows on the east wall, just a sliding glass door leading to our bedroom.

Each of those walls are part of the same room. If I'm only looking at one side, it's like I'm looking at a photograph and missing the complete picture. Seeing other points of view provides a better understanding of all the aspects of the topic.

Confronting fear of being wrong, deep-seated insecurity, and fear of abandonment if others disagree with my viewpoint has helped me develop self-confidence. Now, I see the perspectives of others as enriching my understanding instead of viewing them as a threat.

6. DEMANDING

When people won't listen to me (especially my kids), I don't know how to ask for what I want, or I fear not getting what I want, it's easy to become demanding.

Once I'm aware of using this unhealthy approach, I can check out *Parenting with Love and Logic*'s "Turn Your Words to Gold," https://www.loveandlogic.com/pdfs/goldhome.pdf for ideas on how to change wording. Also, reviewing the path to empowerment in Chapters 9 and 11 can help me figure out how to communicate what I want or need in a less dictatorial way.

7. MANIPULATING

We learn early how to manipulate through begging, pleading, guilting, and throwing tantrums. To the extent that those tactics worked when we were kids, we continue to employ them as adults. The driving fear underlying this revolves around lack of knowledge of how to get needs met in any other way.

What's a way to shift this? Developing more direct approaches and honest ways of communicating helps us let go of manipulation. See Chapter 9 for ideas on how to do that or try Relationship Enhancement or CoupleTalk.

8. CRITICIZING

As children, we learn to be judgmental from our role models. If they criticized us, we learn to be critical of others.

How can we stop this? In Chapter 12, we talked about combating negativity by consciously choosing to look for the good and commenting on that instead of pointing out failures, flaws, and faults. Problems still need to be addressed, of course, but if the concern is sandwiched between positive affirmations, it's easier for the person being corrected to accept and receive the admonition in a more positive spirit.

Our critical attitude towards others masks our own underlying fear of being unlovable. Picking at the flaws of others is driven by feeling overwhelmed by our own imperfections. Putting others down to lift ourselves up backfires. We deflect from our shortcomings when pointing out the mistakes of others. At the same time, when we slime others with criticism, internally we feel bad without realizing it. Both the giver and receiver of judgmental remarks lose. Plus, it erodes love and affection.

Knowing I'm loved and accepted fully by God, in the core of my being, fills me with love and acceptance of myself, making it possible for me to be loving and accepting of others. Often, it is necessary to seek the help of a counselor skilled at addressing trauma. Some effective methods include EFT, art therapy, experiential approaches, psychodrama, EMDR, music therapy, narrative therapy, equine therapy, gestalt, and sand tray.

9. CONTROLLING

Often, our attempts to control others stem from a desire to make the world feel safe. I tell others what to do because I feel powerless to make changes for myself. What I fail to see is that I'm only partially successful in my approach. Others may comply with my wishes, but it doesn't gain me the love and acceptance I crave. At best, others begrudgingly comply. My ordering people around just makes them pull away emotionally and often physically, too.

What's the alternative?

Learning what I have power over frees me from my compulsive need to tell others what they need to do. There are only five things I can truly control—what I **D**o, my **A**ttitude, my **R**eaction, my **T**houghts, and what I **S**ay (DARTS). They are listed on the fingers of one hand as shown in the following illustration.

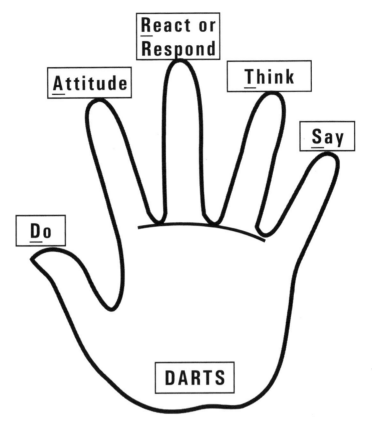

My thoughts control the other four, driving what I do, my attitude, my reaction, and my words. I'm able to let go of fear and powerlessness when I can figure what my next move will be in any given situation. That's why a close relationship with God is so imperative. When we don't know what to do, He gives us wisdom when we ask (James 1:5, CEV).

Once we are aware, we can work on changing what we **do** that is detrimental to others and ourselves. If we feel controlled, angry, or like a victim, we can work on changing our **attitude**. If our **reactions** stink, we can take the necessary time to consider how to respond differently in the future. If our **thoughts** run negative, we can learn to combat them with truth. If someone says something hurtful, I can learn how to speak up, what to **say**, and how to say it in a better way.

Of course, this is much easier said than done and requires determination and practice. We free up the other person, and feel more grounded ourselves, when we learn to work at only controlling self instead of trying to manage others.

10. BEING VOCAL ABOUT FEELINGS AND WANTS

For the things a me-focused person feels strongly about, expressing thoughts, feelings, concerns and desires is easy.[1] On the topics I'm MF about, it's easy for me, too. This isn't as much about feeling powerless as it is about unwittingly driving OFs off the road by our outspokenness.

How can we do this differently?

When we make sure we draw out the feelings and wants of others (in addition to expressing our own views) we both end up on the road. It's important to continue expressing what we think and feel, but make sure we're not silencing others in the process.

Often, others need more time to process and put words to what they're thinking and feeling. MFs can learn to be patient, encouraging of their partners, and willing to give them time to think through before sharing. My daughter-in-law is really good at doing this with my youngest son, giving him time to think and process. Practicing good listening skills proves invaluable for both parties.

11. HAVING HIGH EXPECTATIONS

We all have expectations about different things. These expectations come from the norms we learned in childhood. Identifying, examining, evaluating, and clearly expressing them helps guard against disappointment.

It's fine to have expectations, but important to know what they are. And if we have expectations of others, it's important to express them. If I give my kid money to buy something and expect him to bring home the remaining money, it needs to be clear that's what I want. Otherwise, he'll think it's okay for him to use the difference to buy candy and won't understand why I'm upset that he didn't bring home change.

Too often, I *think* I've expressed my expectations clearly, but they were unclear to my recipient. Asking the other person to repeat what I said helps ensure we both are on the same page. Most of the time, others do want to comply with our wishes if they're expressed in a respectful, non-demanding way.

The hidden-to-ourselves beliefs about how things "ought to be" bite us when they rear their ugly head. If I expect you to give me a card for my birthday but don't make it clear that's what I want, you may be oblivious, but that doesn't keep me from being mad at you for not living up to my secret expectations.

I realize the unrealistic nature of my thought patterns when I put words to my hidden expectations. For example, if I want someone to send me a birthday card, I can say, "It means a lot to me to receive birthday cards. I feel loved when people do that." Or "Words of affirmation is one of my love languages; I feel loved when I receive cards." Or "It meant a lot to me when you sent me a card last year. I like getting cards from you, especially for special occasions."

12. BEING DISAPPOINTED

Close on the heels of expectation follows disappointment. They can't be separated.

How do we guard against that?

The first alternative is to understand and evaluate our expectations. For example, if I go into a high-end French restaurant envisioning being given a massive plate of food, I'm going to be shocked by the small portions.

Another possibility involves changing the meaning I attach to others not doing something I want. Let's continue with the example above about cards. If someone does *not* send me a card, I need to change the meaning I assign to their action (or inaction). I might be tempted to assume they don't love me, while the reality might be that they simply don't value cards the way I do. We need to look to God for the love we want, and not depend on others for that. I need to forgive others when they don't live up to what I wanted them to do for me.

I went zip lining in Thailand on our last trip. Thankfully, I had no expectations of what the experience was going to be like. They didn't tell me, and I didn't ask. If I had expected to start at the top of a mountain and zig zag through the forest downhill all the way, I may have been very upset.

Luckily, my knees are strong, a requirement to navigate the super steep uphill climbs we had between zip lines. Since I had no expectations, I enjoyed life without OSHA's strict rules. We smiled at stairs with no guard rails, 20 percent uphill-grade sidewalks, and stairs with uneven steps. Had I expected American standards, I would have had a miserable time.

Choosing to let go of the way I expect things to be in different countries helps me appreciate what I have at home, gives me a smile at the innovations elsewhere, and sets me free from disappointment.

13. BEING ANGRY

Naming the underlying fears and choosing to resolve them dissipates the anger. It's a process. Many options listed in Chapter 16 can help, especially if you've been living with low-grade anger all your life that occasionally erupts. Resolving anger also involves a lot of forgiveness work. It is possible to live anger-free most of the time. It's worth the effort to get to that place. You'll be glad you did, and so will everybody else in your life.

14. DEMEANING

Addressing deep-seated insecurities that drive us to put down others helps release us from this hurtful behavior.

Consciously choosing to act in loving ways towards others helps build our own self-esteem. We may need help from a counselor to get rid of the contempt harbored toward others that covers up our deeply embedded self-loathing.

15. THREATENING

Threats to harm, punish, or take away privileges are fueled by feeling powerless and not knowing what else to do. We've all been guilty of this at some point in our lives; it's just a matter of degree. What can we do instead? Identify where that powerless feeling is coming from, name the fear driving it, then brainstorm what to do differently. This approach will reveal healthier ways to encourage cooperation, reduce conflict, and achieve what we really want without threats. "Turning Your Words to Gold," https://www.loveandlogic.com/pdfs/goldhome.pdf can help us figure out how to express our desires in an empowered way.

16. YELLING

Fears of someone getting hurt, not getting what I want, or others not doing what I want drives my emotions. I react like a volcano, with words erupting in loud bursts, spewing invectives out with increased volume. I hated yelling at my kids but didn't know what else to do when they didn't do what I requested. Therefore, I defaulted to what my parents did to me.

What's the alternative?

Choosing to take a time out to acknowledge fears and identify options can bring peace. Instead of yelling, try speaking very quietly, stopping until the other person stops talking, or taking a time out to calm down. Refer to Chapters 9 and 11 to state what you want in an empowered way or Chapter 16 for more ideas on what to do about the fear behind the yelling. It's amazing how much quicker cooperation happens when a request is made in a healthy way.

17. ATTACKING/ACCUSING

Fears that underlie the desire to attack may be driven by feeling rejected, abandoned, unloved, or wronged. Those are the most common culprits driving our desire to attack or accuse. Refer to Chapter 11 for more details to combat this behavior.

18. BEING RIGID

Strict adherence to rules provides an illusion of control and a sense of safety. That's why so many legalistic churches, governments, and families have so many regulations. The more chaotic life is, the more directives are established to try to keep others in line.

How do we avoid rigidity?

The more we can self-govern, the fewer guidelines we need. If we all loved God above all else (Mark 12:33) and each other as ourselves, there would be no need for any other parameters.

I've been anal about keeping all the receipts from our trips. We only need the ones for tax-deductible expenses, but I've been holding onto all the receipts, including those for exchanging money, incidentals, and gifts.

One day my spouse asked, "What's behind keeping all of those papers?"

The truth is that my motive is so buried, *I don't even know.* Am I afraid of losing control? I need to do some soul-searching to figure that out. Addressing fears is like stretching; we're a lot more flexible afterward. Ask God to reveal what your rule-following is about, and expose the fears lurking underneath.

19. BECOMING ADDICTED

Addiction is like a vehicle I get in to drive away from the part of my life that leaves me feeling powerless and miserable. I don't know how to address my problems in real life, so I use some escape mechanism to forget about that life. Anything can serve as transportation: food, drugs, sex, relationships, gambling, work, play, mindless games, TV, you name it. Addictions alleviate the pain of my past and my inability to connect in the present in a meaningful way with the people with whom I live. We end up addicted because we didn't get a model of how to have a healthy relationship as a child, never felt fully loved or accepted for who we are and turned to self-medication to ease the pain of disconnection.

How do I avoid the trap of addiction?

Seeking counseling, attending 12-step recovery groups, naming, and addressing the fears can help set us free. Learning communication skills and how to create emotionally safe relationships so we can be truly vulnerable with our partner, family, and friends sets us free from addictions. To have safe relationships, we must stop attacking, criticizing, blaming, and defending. We must own our part and stop waiting for others to change to make our life better.

My decision to work on me had the powerful effect of shifting the relational dynamic of my entire family. I finally became the change I had waited for so long for others to make.

20. PHYSICALLY ATTACKING

Deep insecurities often drive the tendency to physically attack others. Fear of not being good enough, being put down, not being lovable, not safe being alone, not loved, not getting one's needs or wants met, fosters anger that leads to physical aggression. Ask God to reveal and heal the imbedded fears and emotional issues. When a situation is triggering or escalates, give yourself a time out to allow time to cool down and figure out the lies driving the behaviors. Obtaining counseling to heal from childhood wounds helps immensely.

21. HARMING OTHERS

When feelings of powerlessness become too overwhelming, people lash out against others verbally, physically, or sexually because they're so out of control of how they feel inside. The fear is so intense that it takes over, resulting in harming or victimizing others, often replicating the victimization the person experienced in their own childhood.

Every time we hurt someone else, it increases our own shame and feelings of being unlovable and unacceptable. We hate ourselves even more than we did before, which only adds fuel to the behaviors we already loathe and can't seem to control. We addressed this in Chapter 6. We *can* stop the cycle. God can do for us what we cannot do for ourselves. We need help. Humbling ourselves to obtain assistance will set us free.

Often people are terrified of facing the past, but the function of that fear is to keep us imprisoned. I think people fear they will have to relive what they've been through already, but that's not true, especially with EFT or several other approaches that get at our subconscious beliefs. It's never too late to change! You, and everyone in your family will be grateful you sought help. It takes a person of character to recognize they need help; fools just keep doing what they've always done, wreaking havoc everywhere they go.

Now that we know how to get out of the ditch and stay out, let's look at what it is like to be on the road.

POINTS TO PONDER:
- Consider typical go-to ditch behaviors
- Identify fears driving those behaviors
- What alternatives can be employed instead?

CHAPTER 15

ON THE ROAD

"We're not like robots.
God promises to guide us through the Holy Spirit,
but He gives us the freedom to make our own decisions."
—Joyce Meyer

oads provide a great metaphor to represent our conscious actions. The road represents balance, consciousness, mindfulness, and awareness. It's the place where I think about what I want and need, while at the same time keeping others in mind. The view is clear, and I can see what's going on from both sides.

On the road, I am in a better position to determine what is best for all involved and can select the best course of action. Following God's nudges challenges me to choose, requiring mindful evaluation of my options in the process—something I can do when on the road, but can't accomplish when stuck in a ditch.

At street level, I can even see those who are stuck in the ditches, have compassion for them, and realize it's not my job to get them out.

By choosing to stay on the road with my actions, it's like I throw a rope to my ditch cohorts, offering a way for them to grab a hold and climb out if they so desire. That's giving them freedom to choose, just like God gives us. He doesn't force us to come out of our ditches, He throws us a rope so we can climb out with His help.

On the other hand, just as I lived unaware of my actions driven by fear, ditches exist beneath the surface of the road, representing subconscious behaviors. Even when I'm on the road, I can get hung up when facing triggering circumstances or topics.

While facilitating a Parent Vision Trip for a World Race squad in Thailand, I gained a new understanding about how the Holy Spirit works and what life on the road with God looks like. The ministry directive for this group involved asking the Lord (ATL) where to go, who to talk to, and what to do. The squad learns to quiet themselves, pray, and listen to God for guidance. Then they go out looking to fulfill the thoughts or images that came to mind during prayer. They often come back with amazing stories of how it all played out. They actively seek out people whose lives God wants to touch and serve in ways He inspires. They practice listening and acting on the promptings of the Holy Spirit to pray for others, ask for healing, share the gospel, or serve in some way.

During my morning Bible study, I happened to read the story of Nicodemus. Jesus tells him, "unless a person submits to this original creation: the *'wind-hovering-over-the-water' creation, the invisible moving the visible,* a baptism into a new life—it's not possible to enter God's kingdom." (John 3:5–6, MSG, emphasis mine).

In other words, listening for promptings of the Spirit is all about allowing the invisible inspiration of God to influence my physical actions, something that others can then see! Wow! What an *aha!* moment.

On our trip, one woman got an image of a yellow umbrella and sensed that God wanted her to talk to someone who had one. It seemed random and out of context for the area. The squad looked for one for a while but saw no open umbrellas anywhere. They eventually came upon a folded umbrella, but she didn't think that matched the image impressed in her brain, so the search continued. Ahead, they spotted an open yellow umbrella! They approached the individual, struck up a conversation, and ended up praying for the man. He expressed deep gratitude and appreciation because he was going through a difficult time, and they had brought him hope and encouragement.

God wants each of us to submit to "the 'wind-hovering-over the-water' creation, the invisible moving the visible." We can't do that very well when we're under the spell of fear in the ditch. Sometimes it's easier to practice in a country far away, free from the people whose opinions we spend too much time worrying about.

A couple days later, I had afternoon tea with a friend in Chiang Mai who had recently faced some significant challenges. She commented, "Things that are invisible are more real than the visible. Anxiety and fear, which I cannot see, are controlling my actions, which I can see." The revelation I had about learning to listen and respond to the invisible promptings of God just took on another dimension!

We are all moved by invisible promptings, either influenced by the Spirit of God or spurred on by the enemy. When we're not aware, negative forces easily sway us, usually in the form of some aspect of fear, masquerading as anxiety, worry, angst, depression, concern, paranoia, obsession, neuroses, anger, guilt, shame, sadness, impulsiveness, addiction, and more.

The more we practice awareness, the more we open ourselves to the influence of the Holy Spirit leading us in positive ways. I'm learning to practice obeying the promptings from God. I confess I'm not as good as I'd like to be at it, even though I've been a believer all my life. My "I want to do it my own way" self often reacts like Jonah did when asked to go to Nineveh. Too often my response is, "Yah, no!" (and then I land in the ditch). Often what I sense God asking me to do seems strange or illogical. Sometimes that is verification that it comes from God, because I would *never* think of it on my own. When I respond to those promptings, I've experienced some amazing results, such as the story I shared of the fulfillment of my husband's dream to visit a coffee plantation. Living on the road, following God's leading, is always full of surprises!

For years I heard pastors exhort, "Be balanced." I'd listen and agree but didn't have a clue how to make that *happen*. Crawling out of the ditch is my journey of learning how to gain the equilibrium for which I had been searching. In this process, I discovered many strengths that develop from the two extremes. While on the road, we can readily access abilities gained from both extremes.

Let's take a look at a few great qualities developed as a result of coming out of each of the ditches.

STRENGTHS OF BEING OTHERS-FOCUSED

Having a bent toward pleasing others includes many healthy traits. OFs care deeply about others and experience joy in meeting their needs. They feel alive and excited about making a difference and want to make the world a better place for everyone. Easygoing and flexible, others-focused people tend not to get easily upset if things don't go their way or as planned. In fact, most of the time it doesn't occur to them to have a plan. OFs don't often struggle with disappointments because they learned early on not to expect to get what they wanted. They enjoy supporting others in their endeavors and are quite willing to follow. OFs love spontaneity.

As an OF, I'm up for adventure and open to trying new things, except barbecued scorpions. I love to host parties and make sure there's plenty of food for everyone. Giving gifts and bringing smiles gives me joy. I'd rather live in a mediocre house and drive an older vehicle so I can afford to travel the world and impact others in a positive way.

People in service industries tend to be others-focused. They throw great parties and make awesome teachers, wise counselors, compassionate nurses, competent doctors, passionate missionaries, great authors, and engaging servers. Examples include Jesus, Billy Graham, Florence Nightingale, Louis Pasteur, Mother Theresa, and Anne Sullivan.

STRENGTHS OF BEING ME-FOCUSED

Me-focused people likewise develop just as many strong attributes. They tend to be goal-oriented, driven, motivated, focused, and make good leaders. They know what they want and go after it. They aren't burdened with trying to guess what others might want, which makes it much easier to be decisive. They are not weighed down with trying to make everyone else happy, which leaves space for more creativity. When me-focused, it's easier to be single-minded. People readily follow those who have a plan and know where they are going.

Their drive to become the best at their skill leads to world class athletes, musicians, pastors, builders, scientists, artists, inventors, politicians, farmers, and business owners, to name a few. They persevere, take risks, and challenge themselves and others to achieve a higher standard. They are gamechangers, leading the way into uncharted territory. Examples include Jesus, Christopher Columbus, Mahatma Gandhi, Winston Churchill, Amelia Earhart, Emily Dickinson, and Martin Luther King.

You may notice that Jesus shows up on both sides because He was perfectly balanced.

The strengths listed above are by no means comprehensive. When on the road, I manifest the skills I have picked up from time spent in both ditches. When mindful, I can navigate between others- and me-focused tendencies appropriately and seamlessly. Jesus provides us with a perfect example in every action He took, including His choice to give up His life for us. On the road, I know in which circumstances to lead and when to follow.

The predominately others-focused people in the service industry got good at what they do by spending time in the me-focused ditch acquiring skills. Likewise, we all benefit from the talents shared and leadership provided by me-focused people because they did time in the others-focused ditch.

On the road, I can see the fear driving my old ditch behaviors that so frequently crept into my everyday life. More and more, I choose to respond instead of reacting. Learning ways to address the fears that constantly bombard me empowers me.

Now that we have examined some of the strengths honed from time spent in each ditch, in the next chapter, we turn our attention to what to do about fear.

POINTS TO PONDER:
- In what areas of your life are you on the road?
- What strengths did you gain from being Others-Focused?
- What abilities grew out of being Me-Focused?

CHAPTER 16

WHAT TO DO ABOUT FEAR

"The brave man is not he who does not feel afraid,
but he who conquers that fear."
—Nelson Mandela

Now let's get busy and root out those fears that drive our ditchy behaviors and keep us stuck in the ditch. Below, you will find a menu of options for addressing fears once they have been named.

Sometimes trying several things at once may help in getting rid of those nasty anxieties. For instance, when I'm facing fear about having to do something I've never done before, praying about it, choosing to learn about the topic, and discussing it with others will do wonders to shrink the ogre of fear. If I'm trying to decide which job offer to accept, praying about it, discussing it with others, and looking at the pros and cons dispels fear of making the wrong choice.

Here are 24 actions you can take to identify and eliminate the fears that mess with your life.

1. PRAY ABOUT IT

For someone who believes and trusts God to help, this is a no-brainer. However, I noticed how often the feeling of powerlessness creeps in, and that it even blocks my belief that prayer can help. I often don't even think to pray when the situation seems overwhelming, especially when it seems hopeless.

For example, after witnessing the solar eclipse in Wyoming in 2017, we decided to head home that night, along with thousands of others who also thought it was a good idea to "beat the traffic." Our vehicle added one more set of lights to an endless ribbon of bumper-to-bumper taillights tying Northern Wyoming to Denver, Colorado. Around midnight, the driver ahead of us started weaving from side to side.

My first reaction: fear! I commented to my husband, "I'm afraid that driver will cause a wreck in front of us."

Then I thought about ways to face this fear, and it occurred to me. *I can pray and ask for God to intervene!* So, I did. The car stopped weaving! So many other times I did not think to pray for help, maybe because I didn't really believe God would step in.

When events seem too overwhelming, I also forget to pray. The devastation left after hurricanes, earthquakes, or government elections comes to mind. However, our prayers *do* make a difference, even if I can't see the effects immediately. Imagine the change possible if everyone who felt powerless and didn't think to pray in the past decided to start praying!

Any time a situation seems overwhelming, I feel helpless to do something, or I can't make someone else do something, I can pray and ask God to intervene. I then need to confront my fear that God won't do it the way I think He should do it in the time frame I think it should be done. It *will* happen, in God's way and in His time.

2. TALK ABOUT IT; GET INPUT FROM OTHERS

Discuss the issue with others, and get input from several people. This does *not* necessarily mean that you have to do what they recommend. However, if two or three people recommend something opposite of what you want to do, it might be wise to listen.

A couple of important points to remember: 1) consider with whom you discuss the topic, and 2) consider how you frame it.

Perhaps your marriage is difficult, and you want to know what to do. Seeking input from divorced drinking buddies might not provide the best guidance, unless you ask them about their regrets and what they realize now that they didn't see before.

The Bible tells us, "Without good direction, people lose their way; the more wise counsel you follow, the better your chances" (Proverbs 11:14, MSG). Discuss the following questions with others: What is your dilemma? What questions do you have about the situation? Where do you feel stuck? Who has been through something similar in which you desire the kind of outcome they achieved? Whose judgment do you trust?

How I talk about it also affects the outcome. In my old ditchy way of doing things, I'd discuss it, but with all the wrong people. That's called complaining and gossiping. While that *is* talking about it with others, it's not for the purpose of figuring out what to do. That approach comes from a desire for someone to feel sorry for poor me based on my belief that I was powerless to do anything myself. I avoided approaching the person with whom I most needed to discuss the issue. Fear of the reaction I'd get kept me from addressing it head-on.

A big part of my unsatisfactory results had to do with how I framed what I said. I spoke in terms that caused others to become defensive. I was the queen of the ABCDs discussed in Chapters 10 and 11. I didn't know the path to empowerment. Gaining the courage to stand up to others, even if they don't like what I have to say, is a process. It's challenging. I'm still learning ten years later. But it is worth the effort! Shifting how we do life is an ongoing process. We can't handle all this new knowledge at one time. Trying to incorporate at once all the things you recognize that need changing is overwhelming. Learning bit by bit may take many years, but the trajectory of your life and the positive impact it will have on your family is worth pursuing for the rest of your life. How long have you been in the ditch? It may take that many years to completely turn your ship around, but every move you make in the right direction brings a positive reward.

Going directly to the people involved and approaching the topic from an empowerment perspective helps immensely when I do it in the right way. Review Chapters 9 and 11 for ideas on how to frame your words more effectively.

3. BRAINSTORM FOR NEW OPTIONS; EVALUATE WHAT WORKS BEST

In my family of origin, brainstorming looked like this: Someone suggests an option. Another points out the flaws. A second idea is expressed, only to be met with, "We've tried that before, and it didn't work." A third suggestion is proffered, followed quickly by a disparaging remark. And that's the end of new ideas. That's not brainstorming; it's skeet shooting! Someone launches an idea, and it gets shot down.

True brainstorming looks much different. *Every* idea that comes to mind gets recorded, no matter how ridiculous it sounds. Whether done individually or in a group, the brainstorming process looks the same. Any idea that comes to mind gets written down. Someone suggests: "Let's get on a rocket ship and go to the moon." You know that's not a viable option. There's not enough money, nor is there a rocket. But it is included in the list of ideas, even though it obviously won't work. Why write it down? Because it keeps the ideas coming. It communicates freedom to be creative and think outside of the box. Maybe a great idea or solution will stem from the crazy suggestion.

Once I have exhausted all thoughts regarding the topic and every suggestion has been jotted down, only then do I cross off the ones that don't apply to the situation. Then, I examine the pros and cons of ones that remain, which leads me to the next point.

4. MAKE A LIST OF PROS AND CONS FOR EACH OPTION THAT HOLDS MERIT

So many times, fear of making the wrong decision paralyzed me. That's why it took me thirty years to figure out what I wanted to do when I grew up. Now, when faced with choices, I make a list of all the pros and cons.

I used to feel stuck again when the positives equaled the negatives, but I've since learned to rate each one on a scale from 0–10. That helps clarify how much value I place on each of the reasons for and against a given point.

For example, when presented with a job offer, aspects to consider included:

Pros	Cons	
8	—	Commute distance
5	—	Type of job
7	—	People I will be working with
6	—	Pay rate
—	-4	Opportunity for advancement
—	-8	Benefits package
—	-2	Vacation time
6	—	How much I enjoy the work
32	14	

When I rated these points, and then added up the total for each position, the pluses far outweighed the minuses. If I have two options, I'd examine the advantages and disadvantages of each. That helps me see the most favorable path. This tactic works for anything to do with making choices, whether it be which school to attend, where you'll land on your next vacation, or which house to buy.

As a result of consciously thinking through all aspects of an issue, fear of making the wrong choice goes away.

5. IDENTIFY THE LIE, ACCEPT THE PIECE THAT IS TRUE, AND REJECT THE REST

What people say can be very hurtful. It cuts the deepest when there's an element of truth. For me, that includes: "You're always late!" and "You're wrong again!" A little voice inside agrees. Then guilt and shame rush in. In this situation, it helps to sort out what is true and what is not. Being on time is not my strong suit. So, what's the lie in that comment? The lie is that I'm *always* late. I'm on time when I need to be, most of the time. So, accepting the truth, "I'm late this time," and rejecting the lie that it is "always," puts the situation in perspective.

The same is true for "You're wrong again!" This one is a little more subtle. It can be true that I've made an error, but in this case, the little voice inside takes that truth and runs with it. I self-condemn with, *There, you screwed up again. You're always blowing it; you'll never get it right.* I become my own worst enemy. I don't need anyone to put me down; I do a fabulous job all on my own. When I confront the lies that attach to an aspect of truth, the level of fear and shame I experience lessens.

I've always looked for verification of what I believe to be true, although I didn't realize it. For many years, I believed I was ugly. I could not accept a compliment from anyone who said I was attractive. If they complimented me, my inner voice contemptuously informed me, *Of course they are complimenting you; they're only interested in what they can get from you. They don't really mean it.* The lie that I'm ugly caused all comments to the contrary to be sent to the automatic delete pile. It was true that I'd never win a beauty contest, but I'm also far from being an ogre. I've finally learned to accept the truth that true beauty is not derived from facial appearance but from the Spirit of God that shines through us. *That* is true beauty. Believing the lie resulted in my misinterpretation of the intentions of others. This contributed to my low-self-esteem and belief that I could never have what I wanted. It also hindered me from doing anything about my inner or outer natural beauty. If you believe you're not attractive, you may wear ill-fitting clothing or an unbecoming hair style and carry yourself in an unappealing way. Inner ugliness shows up when we say caustic and mean things to others.

6. IDENTIFY THE LIE AND COUNTER WITH THE TRUTH

This is another way to attack lies. Lies such as, "I'll never amount to anything," "I can't do anything right," "Nobody loves me," and "I'm not good enough" attack our inner character. They bring with them a feeling of hopelessness. Experiences I had growing up convinced me of the "truth" of those statements. Rarely are comments like that completely true. Let's see what truths we can use to combat those lies.

"You'll never amount to anything" could be countered with "with God, I will accomplish His purpose for my life." It may be true that you haven't amounted to much, *yet*. But with God all things are possible. I never thought I'd travel to the places I've gone or write a book! I once lived as though those lies were true.

During that phase, I didn't amount to much, but God is doing some amazing things in me! You, too, can overcome that curse (and lie) that got passed down to you. If you **decide** you'll amount to something, **you will**.

Many authors and inventors live their lives in obscurity only to become famous *after* they died, such as Van Gogh, Mozart, Emily Dickinson, Edgar Allan Poe, and Galileo. We don't know what God is doing in our lives or the role He influences us to play in the lives of others. So even if *we* can't see or understand what God is accomplishing in our lives, by deciding to believe that He is accomplishing something good in and through us, we squelch that lie that we'll never amount to anything.

"I can't do anything right." Here I see the extreme show up again. I counter this lie with the truth that I did lots of things right. They just didn't get noticed. Only the things I did wrong hit the spotlight.

"Nobody loves me." Negative interactions with parents, siblings, or friends open the door for this lie to sneak in. I remember telling myself this lie as a child. Sometimes I admitted it out loud. More often, I kept that lie locked up securely in my heart, away from my conscious awareness. Then I lived as though it was true, subconsciously pushing away or self-sabotaging any relationship contradicting my false belief. Because I'd concluded that no one loved me, I didn't love myself either. Countering that lie with "God loves me, and I choose to love myself" helped pry loose the grip of the false belief. Over time, I discovered that lots of people love me; I just couldn't accept their love before because I didn't feel worthy.

These negative beliefs probably got passed down for generations, inspired by the enemy to keep my family and me from being all God created us to be. But "God can do anything," and that's the truth for me to cherish (Matt. 19:26, CEV). Even if people don't notice or comment on what I do right, I can start noticing and affirming myself. That sets me free from dependence on others for approval.

Sometimes I need help figuring out how to counter the negative belief. The lie seems so true that I struggle to identify a truthful opposing statement. In that case, I need help from others or a counselor to figure out what will effectively combat the misbelief.

7. CHANGE YOUR STORY

While this is akin to countering the lie with the truth, statements we repeat to ourselves over and over are part of our running commentary, whereas the former point is more situational. Maybe I just need to say it several ways to internalize the point that what I tell myself can either help or hurt me, and the negative things are driven by fear and lies.

I have a story I tell myself about any situation. Lots of times it's a positive one. For example, I prod myself: "I can do this," or "A stranger is a friend I haven't met yet."

However, I also have stories I whisper internally based on wounding from my past: "I'm stupid." "I'll never get what I want." "This [bad situation] always happens to me." "I'm a victim." That's the negative story I tell myself that I want to change. Those statements *feel* true, but they're not.

When I have a negative experience that touches on that wounding, it reinforces the story that keeps playing in my head. For example, so many times I've lamented, "Other people get to have really nice things, but I can't," "I can't spend money on myself," or "No one will ever love me." Because I believed those things, I didn't even attempt to pursue the desires I held in my heart. This may come from a generational spirit of poverty. Or something happened to convince me that I could not have (fill in the blank). As a result of that conviction, unwittingly I deprive myself.

In the animated movie *Inside Out* a red toy train is called, "the train of thought." That image provides a great visual representation. It reminds me of when Paul said, "take every thought captive" (2 Cor. 10:5, ESV). I never knew how to do that until I saw that movie and realized that I'm the conductor of the train of thought that runs in my head all the time. Since I am in charge, I can pull the stop cord whenever I want and check what's in each of the cars. On my first investigation, I discovered that most of the cars were filled with negative self-talk. From then on, I worked on replacing one negative belief at a time with a new story. "I'll never have what I want" shifted to "I can seek God to obtain what I want. If it's within His will, I will have it." "I can't do that" switched to "I can do all things through Christ who strengthens me." (This book is getting done! Before, I felt overwhelmed by the task) "This always happens to me" got reframed to "this has happened often, but I no longer identify with that." "I'm a victim," changed to "I am no longer a victim; I'm thriving."

8. FIGURE OUT WHAT YOU CAN DO AND DO IT

Perhaps this one is obvious, but fear causes us to freeze, resulting in inability to take action. Remember that demons are limited in what they can do to us. Their favorite tactics include scaring and discouraging. Imagine I'm climbing a ladder lined by demons shouting all kinds of condescending and scary remarks. As I advance, they try to get me to slow down, stop in confusion, or give up and quit. I do that when I believe their lies and don't continue forward movement. I combat that by examining what I'm afraid will happen and consciously taking action to prevent it. If I'm afraid I'll run out of gas, I can ensure I never let the tank get below a quarter full. If I'm afraid I'll fail a test, I can make a plan to study a little every day or get help to understand the difficult concepts. Fear of not having enough money for something can be thwarted by praying for God to provide and help align my spending with what I value most. It's empowering to face fear head-on. Think about what you can do to resolve the fear; then do it.

9. RE-PRIORITIZE IF NECESSARY

When feeling overwhelmed with all that needs to be accomplished, make a list of all the tasks weighing on you. Next, evaluate which one needs to be done first and tackle that, ignoring the rest of the items until that task is complete. We can only do one thing well at a time.

10. FACE THE FEAR AND DO IT ANYWAY

Sky divers, rock climbers, and tower-of-doom riders have mastered this point. They experience fear but do it anyway! The rest of us would do well to follow suit. Just be sure to calculate and make the risk reasonable. No jumping off cliffs without a bungee!

On a more day-to-day level, taking a risk might look like responding to a nudge from the Holy Spirit to talk to a stranger, pray for a coworker, or donate to a charity. Fear rushes in, whispering, "What will they think if I do that?" "Will the coworker reject me?" "I don't have enough money to do that." Ask God for confirmation and then step out in faith.

At this writing, I'm in Thailand at a hotel. Three times I shared the elevator with a traveler from Taiwan. During each ride we exchanged pleasantries. On my third trip heading down with him, I felt inspired to ask if I could pray for him, not something I normally do for strangers in elevators. He agreed, then pulled out a Bible to show me that we share the same faith! I've been working on overcoming the fear of praying for random people, and it's rewarding!

11. IDENTIFY THE EXTREMES AND FIGURE OUT WHAT'S IN BETWEEN

For so much of my life, I could only see extremes. Argue or say nothing. Be married and miserable or get a divorce. He gets his desires met, and I don't. I get what I want, and he doesn't. In my black and white thinking, I lacked awareness and could not imagine any options existing in the middle!

It was quite a stretch for me to begin thinking of what the middle ground could look like on a given subject. Instead of arguing vs. silence, I learned to have skilled dialogue. Between married and miserable, I found staying together and getting help or separating and getting help and then reuniting. Instead of being a martyr and giving up what I want or insisting on my preferences, I started identifying underlying positive motivations for our desires and discussing them to discover win-win solutions.

Sometimes we may need help to find the middle ground because we can't figure it out on our own. A professional counselor or coach often has a more objective perspective and can help reveal options we cannot see.

12. IF YOU CAN'T DO ANYTHING ABOUT IT, DECIDE TO LET IT GO

Making a conscious decision to let go of the fear changes the game. For example, if a storm is coming and you have brought in the things that might blow away, secured everything else, and there's nothing more you can do, decide to let go of any fear about what might happen. During Hurricane Irma, my sister and her husband did just that. When it came over them, they listened to the wind howl and the rain pelt down. They had no fear because they decided to let it go and instead trusted God for protection.

A more everyday example is getting stuck in traffic. Often, I leave just enough time to get to where I want to go. When traffic would suddenly slow to a standstill because of an unexpected accident, I tended to get nervous and worried about being late. I'd anxiously look ahead to ascertain how long the delay might be. The whole time, my stomach would be in knots, my palms sweaty on the steering wheel, and my mind racing trying to figure out alternate routes.

Now, I notice the fear that comes up when faced with delays and think about what I can do about it. I call the person I'm supposed to meet and let them know I may be late, then relax and listen to music. Anxiety won't get me there one second earlier. It just steals all enjoyment of the moment. The fear *only* goes away when the decision is conscious. I now decide not to be afraid but rather, confident that things will work out. We can also ask God to stretch time so we can still get there in a timely manner, if needed.

13. LEARN OR EDUCATE YOURSELF ABOUT THE TOPIC

Any time I face something I've never done before, fear accompanies it. The first time I went to college, interpreted at church, traveled internationally, bought a car, purchased a house, had kids, or started a new job, I felt anxious about it. *What did I get myself into?* I'd ask myself. It is scary to do something I've never done before. Perhaps fear of failure, that I won't be competent or good enough to accomplish the task before me drives that feeling. The level of fear decreased significantly as I delved into learning about each new challenge. The more I learned, the less I feared.

14. CHRIST GIVES ME THE STRENGTH TO FACE ANYTHING

We always have God to help through every challenge in life. That also includes when we have screwed up, failed in a big way, or are at fault. When we face difficulties, it's easy to forget that because fear clouds our ability to think clearly. At that point, take a deep breath to get more oxygen to the brain. Then remind yourself, "I can do all things through Christ who strengthens me," (Philippians 4:13 NKJV) including getting through the current crisis.

15. LOOK AT IT FROM GOD'S PERSPECTIVE

Consider: What is God doing in my life through this challenge I'm facing? Sometimes telescoping out to look at your problem from God's viewpoint might help you see the situation in a different light. Think of how your specific trial can be used for good, both in your life and in the lives of others. That includes the icky thing you're going through right now, even if it seems impossible to imagine how good could ever come from it.

Often, challenges refine our character. Through trials we become aware of errors in judgment and things we have been lax about, discover better ways to handle problems, learn to forgive, are prompted to pray for enemies (anyone who comes against me fits in that category), and are stretched in service for others. When I consider how God might be using my challenges to grow me and expand the kingdom, my trial doesn't feel so random.

16. REMEMBER THAT THE END OF THE SITUATION WILL TURN OUT FOR THE BEST

God promises to make *all* things work together for good, even really bad things (Rom. 8:28, CEV). He *will* help you get through it. If things aren't going well, it's not done yet. God doesn't say things will be good at the beginning or the middle, just at the end.

In our lives together, my spouse and I have purchased only one brand new automobile. My husband was driving home from work one day within the first year of owning it. He happened to be behind an asphalt truck, and the rush-hour traffic suddenly slowed, bringing them to an unexpected halt. The only thing that didn't stop was the momentum of the black asphalt in the truck ahead. The tailgate swung open and spilled over, burying the front end of our new red car.

My husband had to pursue the truck to get the driver to stop to gather insurance information. Then we had to file a claim, take our car in to get fixed, and deal with all the inconveniences that brought. Remembering God's promise, I asked, "How is this going to work out for good?" From my vantage point, I couldn't see any potential positives.

Though our car was new, we already had a cracked windshield and a damaged front bumper. Because the asphalt covered the front end, repairs covered those two preexisting conditions. Insurance also covered the cost of a rental while our vehicle was in the shop. We enjoyed driving a sportier model than we owned. Repairs took longer than expected, and we ended up with the loaner for a month, preventing a month's worth of wear and tear on the car we owned. Despite the hassles, we ended up with a car in better shape at no expense to us. And the recommended car repair shop belonged to a family in our church, so they were blessed with the work. God *did* make it all work together for good.

17. ASK YOURSELF: WHAT IS THE WORST-CASE SCENARIO AND HOW LIKELY IS THAT TO HAPPEN?

It's a human tendency to go straight to imagining the worst. When I express my greatest fears, my conscious mind can help the scared little kid inside of me calm down. Assessing the probability of it happening puts a healthy dose of reality around it. Often our fears turn out to be unfounded. Plan how you would address the situation if it were to occur, then decide to stop worrying.

18. USE COPING SKILLS TO CALM DOWN

Sometimes it's necessary to postpone addressing issues for a variety of reasons. Perhaps the season of life and pressures of day-to-day responsibilities consume all of our time and energy. We may not have the bandwidth or financial wherewithal to deal with emotions while at the same time juggling everyday life.

For instance, going through school, raising small children, caring for aging parents, battling a serious illness, or having to work two jobs to make ends meet leaves no room to also work through grieving a loss or being overwhelmed due to a traumatic experience. These things will need to be dealt with at some point, but not now. It's for times like these that ideas for coping in a healthy way come in handy until things calm down enough to address and resolve the issue. For the time being, we just need some space from what troubles us.

Coping methods listed below are grouped into three general categories according to the type of benefit they offer. Some help us calm down, others serve as a distraction, some help us to process what happened. These are stop-gap measures, like a band-aid until the issue can be addressed head-on.

Because we are all unique, some of these might not work for you. It's my hope that the broad variety of options listed provides a springboard to develop options that work well for you. The objective is to find some inner peace despite all that's going on. Each of the following have the potential to benefit depending on the individual and the situation.

Helps you calm down:
    Pray about it
    Meditate
    Journal
    Practice deep breathing
    Listen to uplifting music
    Clean or reorganize an area
    Pamper yourself (massage, pedicure, manicure, new haircut)
    Go for a drive
    Visit family members or friends (who encourage)
    Work out
    Take a coffee/tea/water break
    Read self-help books about the topic
    Take a bubble bath with candles to light the area

Allows time to think about what happened:
    Go to the gym/work out
    Take a walk
    Spend time with animals
    Take a shower or bath
    Sit in a hot tub
    Engage in physical activity

Distracts from what happened:
Socialize
Learn something new
Surround yourself with positive people
Volunteer
Change your environment
Take time off or go on vacation
Read
Engage in a hobby
Create something (craft cook, paint, sew, build)
Watch TV or a movie
Buy a new outfit
Do something fun
Go to an event
Plan a trip
Go out to eat
Engage in a sport
Play a video game
Watch a sport or event
Drive go-carts or go to amusement park
Go to the recreation center
Teach someone something
Embark on a service project or donate unwanted items

19. ASK YOURSELF: "HOW COULD THIS BE WORSE?"

Anyone who has experienced loss through fires, floods, hurricanes, tornadoes, or typhoons knows how hard it is to pick up the pieces and begin rebuilding a shattered life. Sometimes it's an emotional disaster instead. Relational storms invade our lives, ripping apart families, friends, and faith. We're left feeling like a twister ripped through our life, leaving nothing but a pile of rubble. As much as we'd like to crawl into a hole and die, we must go on.

Looking at how our circumstances could be worse than they are diminishes our tendency to "awfulize." It helps us see the positive and count blessings instead of throwing a pity party, which becomes critical when we experience something devastating. When we look at how things could be worse, we see a ray of hope to combat the despair that threatens to engulf.

20. JOURNAL

Journaling in all its various forms provides an invaluable means to get thoughts on paper and out of our heads so we can step back to gain a more objective view. Sometimes doing a "brain dump" works. Write down everything that comes to mind about a topic, then go back and review what has been written.

Another strategy is to write down thoughts and then ask for God's input on them, writing what comes to mind in a different color. Seth Barnes's excellent book *Listening Prayer* provides more details on this topic.[1]

You might explore your assumptions by identifying what happened, what you assumed was true about it, what you believed the other person's motivation was behind their actions, and the feelings you have about it. Naming your feelings brings understanding about your reactions. Examining these four parts individually raises consciousness, pulling you out of the ditch, where you feel stuck and powerless, and onto the road.

Another type of journaling called, Immanuel Journaling, provides yet another way to get at what's going on while seeking God's perspective on the issues. A downloadable worksheet is available at: https://www.soulshepherding.org/immanuel-journaling-worksheet/. I've found this method to be enriching and enlightening.

Some hesitate to journal because of fear their privacy will be invaded. Name that fear, and then figure out what to do about it. Perhaps storing your journal in a locked cabinet, in your car, or another place to which only you have access may be necessary.

21. DO EFT ON IT

We are fearfully and wonderfully made by God (Psalm 139:14, KJV)! God created neuro-network endpoints at strategic places in our bodies. Thinking about what is disturbing and tapping on those points at the same time stimulates the brain and helps it process the information. Our nervous system calms down, and we feel much better, often in a very short amount of time.

Gary Craig, who developed Emotional Freedom Technique, says to try it on everything![2] A friend took that suggestion seriously and tried it before bowling. Instead of bowling a typical low-scoring game, he got several strikes in a row! I've used it to address countless issues: lies, fears, negative beliefs, traumatic memories, grief, sadness, anger. I've used it to improve my ability to ski and bike ride; improve flexibility; eliminate allergies; increase positive affirmations; clear out headaches, migraines, sore throats, aches, and pains; come to a place of forgiveness; and more. It's an amazing tool, especially when you include prayer and focus on forgiveness of self, others, and God for allowing our difficult circumstances.

However, it took me a year to accept EFT as a valid approach because it was so far outside of my paradigm of how healing occurs. While still doubting its effectiveness, I kept using it and being surprised with what it accomplished. EFT is like the mud Jesus made when He spit on the ground and made a paste to rub on the blind man's eyes (John 9:6–11, CEV). Did Jesus need to do that to heal the man? Of course not! Sometimes, we need something to help get our own doubts out of the way so God can work. I had lots of objections to using EFT at first, but eventually overcame them and am so glad I did! EFT enables us to actively participate in God's healing work.

With EFT, I acknowledge the truth of what I think and feel, even when I secretly believe a blatant lie. EFT brings buried thoughts, feelings, beliefs, and fears to the surface, and helps us accept ourselves and forgive others and ourselves. God is my healer; EFT is just a tool, like taking medication.

22. GO TO COUNSELING

I went to a church that also decried the use of therapists. If someone had a problem, they looked to the pastor for help. The church dealt with serious issues like alcoholism, infidelity, smoking, and other problems by excommunication. That only served to convince people to mask their issues and avoid seeking outside help to address them. As a result, it never occurred to me to seek professional help for the grief I experienced for my losses as a teen or for my marital difficulties.

Only after that church fell apart because of major doctrinal changes, and I sank in hopelessness and despair to the point of wanting to end my life, did I seek out the help of a counselor. Thirty years after the sudden losses of my grandmother and brother, I finally began to heal. Unbeknownst to me, the emotions and grief stayed with me, unresolved, that whole time. Time does *not* heal all wounds, as I had been told, unless they are actively addressed. Also, because of the lies, fears, and negative beliefs that became embedded as a result of those deaths, I made a lot of bad decisions, which could have been avoided had I gotten help in a timely manner.

An effective therapist can help you process through your issues; find peace; improve your relationships; and resolve problems that haunt you, leaving you feeling trapped, powerless, sad, angry, and alone. From my perspective, therapy consists of talking about issues and getting an outside perspective, learning new ways of addressing problems, communicating more effectively, and doing trauma healing work using approaches that get at the beliefs held in our subconscious.

Psychology Today offers an extensive list of therapists, searchable by location, on their website; or you can search for "Christian therapist near me" or for the type of therapist you desire. Your insurance company may also have a list of in-network providers to help you find a suitable counselor. Or you can search for a life or relationship coach who can help you move forward.

23. ATTEND A RECOVERY GROUP

Joining a recovery group did wonders for my spouse and me. There are many types of groups available both online and in person. The most famous, of course, are Alcoholics Anonymous (AA) and Al Anon. Sex Addicts Anonymous, Gamblers Anonymous, Narcotics Anonymous, and Overeaters Anonymous have also gained popularity; and there are many others as well. These are all based on the twelve steps to recovery established by AA.

Celebrate Recovery is a nationwide Christian group offering a Biblically based adaptation to AA's approach. They focus on helping Christians with their "hurts, habits, and hang-ups" no matter what their issues are.[3] For a long time, I volunteered at our church's recovery program and used to tell newcomers, "If you have a belly button, you have issues, and this program can help." Then I met someone who didn't have a belly button! However, that person admitted to having issues, too; so, I guess it can help everyone.

The recovery program helped me in several ways. For the first time in my life, I discovered that I wasn't alone in my problems. Instead of rejection and condemnation, which I had previously experienced from my family and some church attendees, I received love and acceptance after sharing the dark side of me. During group time, attendees divulged their story for three to five minutes at a time, so it was manageable to let out our struggles little by little. When I talked about what swirled around in my mind, I had a chance to more objectively view my thought process. What made so much sense in my head didn't seem nearly as logical once expressed verbally. I had freedom to change what I thought through sharing! Group guidelines mandated no "fixing" (telling others how to solve their problems) or advising and strict confidentiality, along with a few other stipulations, which created a sense of safety for the group.

Counseling and attending recovery groups helped me heal from life's hurts and massively improved my life, happiness, and peace. My spouse and I also gained tools for addressing problems more effectively and learned communication skills that provided us with a framework for discussing even the most volatile and difficult issues without ending up in an escalated argument.

24. IN THE NAME OF JESUS CAST IT OUT

"God has not given us a spirit of fear" (2 Tim 1:7, NKJV). I read that verse many times over the years but never picked up on what this really meant. According to that verse, what is fear? It's a spirit!

What!?!

I always thought it was an emotion, how I felt. While I do *feel* fear, this verse tells me it is a spirit. Things that are invisible are more real than the visible. Things we *can't* see, such as anxiety, fear, and powerlessness on the negative end, and love, faith, and trust on the positive end drive and control the actions we *can* see. Once I become aware that fear has been lurking in the shadows, I can do something about it.

So, I tell my anxiety, worry, angst, fretting, and fear to go packing, repent for allowing it to steal my joy, then in the name of Jesus cast it out and replace it with trust that God will take care of me. The "fear spirit" makes me believe that holding onto it in some way helps, protects me from what I'm afraid will happen, or prepares me to accept anticipated bad news. But it does none of those things. It only steals my peace and joy from the moment I feel the fear until the minute the event I'm living in fear about either does or does not happen. About 50 percent of the time, the thing I fear doesn't even materialize! Therefore, all that time spent dreading what might happen was for nothing! And if what was feared does happen, it means having the fear didn't prevent it!

Now let's shift our attention to consider what qualities to look for in an ideal relationship.

POINTS TO PONDER:
- Which of the 24 ways to overcome fear do you want to start practicing?
- Which methods of overcoming fear do you feel like you have mastered?
- What is one fear you want to focus on overcoming?

CHAPTER 17

DEVELOPING AN IDEAL RELATIONSHIP

"I'm not telling you it's going to be easy -
I'm telling you it's going to be worth it."
—Art Williams

When you get into a new relationship, every quality you're hoping the new partner possesses resides, in detail, in your subconscious, but it doesn't make it up the elevator to consciousness. It lies hidden in expectations, hopes, and assumptions that you've already seen all their flaws, they'll never hurt you, or they'll change for you.

Only after the relationship has jostled too far down a rocky road and gotten stuck in a ditch do we stop to evaluate the contrast between the idealized relationship hidden deep within the recesses of our subconscious and the one in real life.

When I was a teenager, my ideal guy description was limited to looks, eye color, height, weight, and the feeling of ve and connection such an apparition evoked. Evaluating other haracteristics didn't even cross my mind.

For most of my life, my vision of an ideal relationship existed nebulously, undefined. I held an internal craving for something ethereal, but never thought to identify the components comprising what I thought a perfect mate would be like. Too many people lament, after yet another failed relationship, "I just want to be happy!"

When asked to describe what would bring about that euphoria, words failed my clients, which got me to thinking about my current state of joy and contentment, feelings that had eluded me most of my life. What was different?

After contemplating what I wanted most in a mate—and many people seeking counsel say they are looking for—I realized that freedom for myself in relationship requires also providing the same things for my partner.

We both need:

- To be loved and accepted for who we are in all circumstances, even at our worst.
- To share our thoughts, feelings, concerns and desires within a framework of safety.
- To attend to our spirit and be aware of what lifts us up and what brings us down.
- To be able to laugh at each other's corny jokes, quirkiness, odd habits, and strange ways of doing things instead of putting the mate down or making fun of the other.
- To be assured that we have each other's best interests at heart.

With that as a backdrop, the following list of qualities emerged that comprise what I consider to be an ideal partner.

Of course, to have an ideal partner, we need to *become one*. It may be helpful to look at the relationship you have now and rate each of these elements to assess what's going well and what needs work. That can provide talking points to discuss with your mate or to work on improving on your own or with a counselor.

These may not be your criteria exactly, but I hope it gives you enough content to develop your own "ideal relationship" list:

To be free to be me, accepted fully with all my faults, flaws, and failures. I want to be loved even when I'm occasionally weird, odd, strange, and curious.

Honesty. I want to know how he's feeling, even if it means he tells me how upset he is with me. That requires me having the emotional maturity to accept that I may have said or done something wrong. I must resist becoming defensive, and that is *hard!* I also want to be honest in the same way. This may take work.

To have fun together. We love to camp, travel, alpine and cross-country ski, watch funny movies, bike ride, and have friends over. Doing fun activities strengthens our relationship.

To have fun separately. If I want to do something and he doesn't, I am free to do it without him. I don't feel guilty or feel like I have to fight for what I want.

For the other person to be free to be themselves. This means I avoid attacking, criticizing, blaming, or telling my mate what to do. I help create that sense of freedom.

To not control. This ties into the point above. Control is the opposite of freedom. I need to be conscious of times I attempt to make things go the way *I* want them to without regard for others. There's nothing wrong with wanting things to go a certain way; it's when the feelings of others are discounted or not taken into consideration that this becomes an issue.

To not be controlled. I also need to stop *allowing* others to control me. I need to be mindful of when things are done out of conscious choice or from feeling like I have no choice. Work to eliminate actions driven out of obligation.

Time alone. I need time alone without feeling guilty about it.

Time separate from my mate. When the relationship is new, we want to be together all the time. But over time, we need space away from each other. Our relationship is richer when we have more going on than living like Siamese twins.

Time with friends with my mate. I want to have friends we both enjoy and to engage in activities together like parties, camping, travel, picnics, and card games. We need social time with friends and with our mate in balance. If you feel like you're being blocked from time with friends by your mate, some changes need to happen. That's not freedom. I need to feel free and not obligated.

To both get through conflict peacefully. That does not mean stuffing down your feelings. It means discussing them and working through the issue, with both sides having a say. Most of us didn't get a good model for working though disagreements without arguing, yelling, leaving, or sweeping it under the rug.

CoupleTalk or Relationship Enhancement programs provide tools to do this.

To be on the same page with my faith. Whether you have a strong or weak conviction, sharing beliefs is more important than you may think. God told Solomon that if he married women from a different faith, they would turn him away from his beliefs. That happened. It's easy to put God second when we find someone who seems to meet our criteria in every other way. However, our gods destroy us. Solomon made women his gods (1 Kings 11:2, KJV) and they eventually destroyed him and his future kingdom (1 Kings 11:31–33, KJV).

To have a passionate relationship that lasts a lifetime. This requires the freedom to be vulnerable, to say no when appropriate, and to feel emotionally safe. With all the wounding from childhood and other relationships, most couples need help in this area.

To get along with most people. It's important to me that my husband does not become aggressive on the road or with other people. This points back to knowing how to get through conflict peacefully. If either one of you struggle with aggression, it points to the need to get help to heal from deep fears and wounds.

To trust. I need to trust that my spouse isn't lying to me or cheating on me. This starts with feeling safe to share thoughts and feelings with one another without judgment or condemnation. If comments are met with "That's stupid," "You don't know what you're talking about," "You're wrong," or other disparaging remarks, that's a giant red flag that this person is not safe. Perhaps not knowing how to create safety is the issue, which can be learned. If words don't match actions early in the relationship, they won't improve without concerted effort as the relationship continues. We all have been guilty of letting those around us down occasionally. The overall pattern reveals whether an individual is trustworthy or not. If we do not act in trustworthy ways, we will pull untrustworthy people into our lives. I had to *learn* to become trustworthy and to trust. Trust is synonymous with faithfulness.

To accept imperfections in my mate without belittling or criticism. I don't want to be belittled or criticized. I need to make sure I don't do that either.

To be happy or joyful. Our joy comes from the Lord (Matt. 25:21, KJV). I desire someone who generally feels positive about life, experiences, and relationships, and pushes through occasional disagreements, things not going as planned, and other hiccups in life.

To express how I feel without criticism or judgment. I want someone with whom: I can express my perspective and feelings. I don't want to be told how I should feel, that I shouldn't feel the way I feel, or that I should just get over it. I don't want to hear how I have it a lot better than others and shouldn't complain, what I ought to do, or how I should fix it.

To accept how the other person feels without criticism or judgment. If I want that for myself, I need to provide it also. I need to accept my mate's feelings without attacking, criticizing, defending, or blaming, even when my partner is upset with me or it was my fault.

To see and be seen. If we didn't feel seen or heard in childhood, chances are we still struggle with feeling unseen and unheard. Learning how to validate ourselves, listen to each other, and reflect what we both hear helps improve this.

To be friends and like each other. We need to like each other and desire to be together and spend time together. Often, when a couple starts out as romantic partners without building friendship first, the relationship falls apart. We need a basis of friendship. If it's missing, it can be built with intention. Love and like are two different things. Both are necessary.

Not to be jealous or demanding. This is part of not trying to control the other person. The person who is jealous reveals insecurity and lack of trust or may have a history of experiencing betrayal. If this is an issue, assistance for healing is available. It's on me to not be jealous or demanding, too.

To have similar life goals. This is important for a lasting relationship. If my husband and I did not hold the same value about travel, I think that would have been the straw to break the camel's back. As it happened, similar life goals pulled us together when everything else fell apart.

To be able to laugh together. As I was busy writing, my husband called from work in a panic saying the police called him to report that our van got hit and they are at our house. He was surprised that they didn't try to call me too. He knew I was in the back of the house and couldn't hear the doorbell. I hopped up and ran outside to see if the cops were still there. By the time I made it past the garage, I realized the van was in the driveway, undamaged, not on the street. . .and that it was April Fools' Day. We both had a good laugh. For too many years, we were far too serious. Cultivate laughter.

To feel heard and understood. This is critical. If you don't know how to do this, learning these skills will change your life for the better! Did I mention CoupleTalk or the Relationship Enhancement program?

To work well together. A critical building block for our relationship involved working well together. When going through difficult times, shared faith, similar life goals, and work compatibility held us together. This may not be necessary for every couple, but it was for us.

To feel safe. In an unsafe world, it becomes critical to intentionally work at creating a safe environment at home. That involves spiritual, emotional, mental, and physical safety. I need to know that I'm not going to be attacked or belittled for what I believe, feel, or think even if it's occasionally wacky. I need to feel physically safe. Many did not experience a safe environment as children and therefore don't know how to have one as adults. If that's the case, getting help to change the circumstances benefits all involved, including the person or people making the environment unsafe.

To respect each other's boundaries. Respecting boundaries directly ties to feeling safe. Sometimes, we can't hold up our own boundaries. If that's the case, we need to learn how to establish the values we claim to espouse. If our boundaries are consistently violated by others, it's time to withdraw from the situation, letting the other person know why you are withdrawing and when you'll come back. If boundaries still aren't respected when you return, ratchet up the length of time you're gone.

Now that you have a list of healthy criteria for a great relationship, rate these factors from 0–100 in your current situation. Low percentages reveal where to start work on improving the dynamics of your interactions:

Perhaps you have some other items you would add. Please do!

Developing an ideal relationship is possible once we define what we're aiming for and act to improve weak areas.

No one is perfect, so start with your current relationship. If the percentages are low for criteria you consider to be deal-breakers, that may help clarify your next steps. Rating these points and working to improve weak areas will assist you in developing the connection you always wanted but didn't know how to achieve.

There are no perfect relationships out there, despite the fairy tales we so fiercely believe. Every relationship is a mixture of strengths and weaknesses; we can focus on improving our good points and reducing the impact of our defects.

POINTS TO PONDER:

- Consider the components that comprise an ideal relationship for you.
- Rate your current relationship on the elements listed.
- What area do you want to improve first?
- What other items would you include to describe your ideal relationship?

AFTERWORD

ROAD TRIP

*"The road to success is not a path you find
but a trail you blaze."*
—Robert Brault

So, where do we go from here?

Perhaps you read this book in a few hours, days, or weeks. Learning how to apply these truths and tools into your relationships, however, is a life-long process and adventure.

If there's anything I hope you take with you from these pages, it's the truth that you're not stuck. You can change how you interact with others, and that will change how they interact with you. You are free to choose. You are empowered. You matter.

After all, the best gift anyone can give is to offer the best version of *themselves* to the world.

Your road trip is beginning. And as you continue to master healthy on-the-road behaviors, keep these things in mind:

God is infinitely greater than any fear you have, and you can overcome all things with His help.

Every person on this planet is a work in progress; forgiving others and ourselves for our mistakes makes us more accepting of others and ourselves.

Practice meditating on good things and giving sincere compliments to everyone in your life.

Choose to forgive yourself instead of judging yourself for not successfully transforming your life the first—or even the fortieth—time that you try.

Practice do-overs with everyone you know.

The less fear we have in our lives, the more we trust God. The more fear we have, the less we trust God.

We are stuck when fear grips us; when God has us, we are free to head down the road.

I wish you joy, freedom, and happiness as you begin to understand and live out what it means to be truly *Unstuck*.

Godspeed on your beautiful journey!

APPENDIX

DITCH BEHAVIORS CHECKLIST

"One man cannot hold another man down in the ditch
without remaining down in the ditch with him."
—Booker T. Washington

*D*itch behaviors stem from the benign to the bizarre. We can easily see what others do to us; it's harder sometimes to catch our own internal enemy.

It may help to highlight in one color in the list below those things that happened to you. Think all the way back to childhood, including how other kids and adults, besides your parents, treated you. Highlight in a different color those things you recognize you have done. If we are honest, everyone will have many behaviors highlighted.

There is *no one* on this planet who can say they avoided experiencing any of these or did not resort to some of these actions at some point in a heated moment. You may even be surprised about some because they have been such an everyday part of your life that they feel completely acceptable. It may be worth pondering why that item made the list and question whether there is validity to including it in the list. I don't expect anyone to agree with everything I say.

Please put the shame aside as you review this list because shame only keeps us locked into our old, hurtful ways, prevents us from having the courage to see the truth, and blocks us from initiating change. The following list expands on the ditch behaviors discussed in this book. Allow this to inform you and help you have a better, happier life by choosing to work on improving how you respond.

Ditchy Behaviors:[1]
Accusing
Affairs
Attacking
Attitude of superiority, dominance, pride (I'm better than you)
Bait & switch (saying you will do something then changing your mind)
Belittling
Biting
Blaming
Blocking access to others
Blocking exit
Bossing
Brandishing a weapon
Breaking bones
Breaking things
Bruising
Causing job loss
Causing suffering intentionally
Choking
Coercion
Concussions
Controlling access to others
Crazymaking (one minute one way, suddenly the opposite)
Criticizing
Cursing at someone
Demanding something then punishing you for doing it

Demanding to know where you are always
Demeaning
Denying input from others
Denying that an incident happened when it really did
Destroying personal property belonging to another
Dishonesty
Disposing of or destroying mementos
Double standards: It's okay for one but not okay for the other
Drinking too much
Drugs
Eavesdropping
Embarrassing others
Evasiveness
False accusations
Forced sex
Forced to stay in one position for an extreme length of time
Gambling (addictive)
Getting close to your face in a menacing way
Getting rid of your child's things without their consent
Grooming (saying nice things, giving gifts with ultimate goal to control in some way)
Hair pulling
Having to account for all your time
Hitting
Humiliation
Hurting or killing pets
Hurting others
Inconsistent – going from one extreme to the other
Intentionally causing pain
Interfering with work
Intimidating
Invalidating someone by interrupting them, saying they shouldn't feel that way, or not allowing to speak
Isolating a person from others
Kicking
Locking someone in a confined space or room
Lying
Making fun of
Manipulating

Menacing looks
Minimizing the seriousness of a situation
Mocking
Name calling (You are lazy, good for nothing, stupid, clumsy, etc.)
Not allowed to go anywhere alone (as an adult)
Not allowed to have your own opinion
Not allowed to say what you think or feel
Not ever allowing others to win
Opening others' mail
Passive-aggressive behaviors
Pinching
Pornography
Punching
Pushing
Put downs
Rape
Refusing to allow medical care for injuries
Restricting access to shared money
Shaming
Slapping
Spanking too hard or too long
Spitting
Squandering family money so there isn't enough for basics
Stalking
Stealing
Swearing at someone
Taking away ID cards (green card, passport, driver's license)
Taking your money or phone
Taunting
Tearing up photos
Threatening gestures, blackmail, or harm
Threatening punishment by God, courts, police, juvenile detention, foster
homes, or relatives
Threats to report you unjustly
Threats to take the children
Throwing objects
Throwing objects directed at a person
Tone
Tying up

Using a welt-producing object to spank
Using children as your confidant inappropriately
Using others as go-betweens
Using weapons (knife, gun, club, stick, etc.)
Violent sex
When you bring up something bothersome, it gets turned back on you
Withholding basic needs, for food, clothing, housing, or school from others
Withholding child support

Self-harming behaviors:
Anorexia
Anything to an excessive degree: eating, exercising, drinking, drugs, sex, gaming, working
Attempting suicide
Bulimia
Cutting
Depriving self of basic needs or enjoyment
Lying in bed or on the couch all day
Numbing out through addictive or repetitive activities
Prescription medicine addiction
Self-injury
Shutting down
Slamming head or body against a wall
Suicidal thoughts
Taking the blame for everything
Threats to commit suicide
Withdrawing
Other:

_____
_____
_____
_____
_____
_____
_____
_____
_____

As your awareness grows, you will notice things others do or you do that should be on this list. Please let me know so they can be included in future versions. One thing is clear, ALL of us have been guilty of saying or doing ditchy things in our lives.

Many of the actions listed above have been so much a part of our everyday lives that we never even stopped to consider their negative impact on ourselves and those we love the most. Now that our eyes have been opened to these automatic reactions, we can consciously change.

What behavior are you choosing to begin eradiating from your life? Here's how:

Start noticing when you do it.

Ask someone to point out for you when you have done it.

Think of a replacement.

Start implementing the new response.

Ask for do-overs the minute you realize the old, automatic way slipped out. . . again.

ENDNOTES

CHAPTER 1

1   Adapted from Scuka, Rob, and Bernard Guerney Jr., "The Relationship Enhancement Model and the 10 RE Skills," National Institute of Relationship, last modified January 21, 2019, http://nire. org.

CHAPTER 3

1   "Fear," Thesaurus, accessed June 10, 2019, https://www.thesaurus. com/browse/fear.

2   Scuka, Rob, and Bernard Guerney Jr., "The Relationship Enhancement Model and the 10 RE Skills," National Institute of Relationship Enhancement, last modified January 21, 2019, http:// nire.org.

CHAPTER 6

1   Brown, Brené, *Daring Greatly: How the Courage to be Vulnerable Transforms the Way We Live, Love, Parent, and Lead* (London: Penguin, 2015).

2   Anas, Brittany, "Here's How Grief Affects Both Our Minds and Bodies," Simplemost, last modified December 6, 2018, https://www. simplemost.com/how-grief-affects-both-our-minds-and-bodies.

3   Manitoba Trauma Information & Education Centre, "Fight, Flight, Freeze Responses," Trauma Recovery, last modified 2013, https:// trauma-recovery.ca/impact-effects-of-trauma/fight-flight-freeze-responses.

CHAPTER 7

1   Carter-Scott, Cherie, "The 10 Rules for Being Human: Cherie Carter-Scott," AdventureWomen, last modified January 7, 2015, https://www.adventurewomen.com/blog/article/10-rules-human.

2   Ranseth, Joseph. "Gandhi Didn't Actually Say 'Be the Change You Want to See in the World.' Here's the Real Quote," Joseph Ranseth, last modified August 24, 2017, https://josephranseth.com/gandhi-didnt-say-be-the-change-you-want-to-see-in-the-world.

3   Adapted from Scuka and Guerney, "The Relationship Enhancement Model."

CHAPTER 8

1   Scuka and Guerney, "The Relationship Enhancement Model."

CHAPTER 9

1   Adapted from Scuka and Guerney, "The Relationship Enhancement Model."

CHAPTER 10

1   Scuka and Guerney, "The Relationship Enhancement Model."

CHAPTER 12

1   "Encouragement is Oxygen to the Soul," Passiton, accessed June 21, 2019, https://www.passiton.com/inspirational-quotes/5008-encouragement-is-oxygen-to-the-soul.

CHAPTER 13

1   Scuka and Guerney, "The Relationship Enhancement Model."

2   Flecky, Don, and Alexandra Flecky, "CoupleTalk," CoupleTalk, last modified March 31, 2019, https://www.coupletalk.com.

CHAPTER 14

1   Adapted from Guerney, Jr., Bernard, Robert F. Scuka, and Carrie Hansen, "Workshops for Couples," The Center for Couples, Families and Children, last modified 2015, http://relationshipenhancement.org/workshops-for-couples.

CHAPTER 16

1   Barnes, Seth, *The Art of Listening Prayer: Finding God's Voice Amidst Life's Noise* (Ashland Press, Gainesville, GA 2005).

2   "Emofree," Gary Craig, and EFT (the Emotional Freedom Techniques)," Learn EFT, Last modified January 19, 2014, https://gettingthru.org/learn-eft/articles/emofree-gary-craig-eft/.

3   Celebrate Recovery Homepage, accessed June 27, 2019, https://www.celebraterecovery.com.

APPENDIX

1   Marshall, Nancy. Adapted from: "INTRO TO DOMESTIC VIOLENCE for Superior Court Self Help Center Staff." California Courts - Home. Last modified 2001. http://www.courts.ca.gov/partners/documents/dvintro1.ppt.

ABOUT THE AUTHOR

CHARLENE BENSON is a licensed professional counselor. She has a private practice in Westminster, Colorado, where she specializes in relationships, trauma, and addictions. She has been using the Ditch People model for more than a decade. This model helps people identify and address extreme behaviors in themselves and others and find new freedom and happiness in their relationships.

Connect with Charlene on Facebook at:

www.Facebook.com/CharleneBensonAuthor